FORGOTTEN
BURIAL

A CRY FOR JUSTICE FROM BEYOND THE GRAVE

JODI FOSTER

Llewel

D1471825

ABOUT THE AUTHOR

Jodi Foster is an author and a TV and radio personality. *Forgotten Burial* is her debut book with Llewellyn Publications; she is also working on two more books (*It's a Matter of Perception* and *Haunted Chico*). Foster's TV credits include being the star of Syfy's *Paranormal Witness* and *The Apartment*. Find her online at http://www.jodifoster.net/.

TO WRITE THE AUTHOR

If you wish to contact the author or would like more information about this book, please write to the author in care of Llewellyn Worldwide, and we will forward your request. Both the author and publisher appreciate hearing from you and learning of your enjoyment of this book and how it has helped you. Llewellyn Worldwide cannot guarantee that every letter written to the author can be answered, but all will be forwarded. Please write to:

Jodi Foster
⁒ Llewellyn Worldwide
2143 Wooddale Drive
Woodbury, MN 55125-2989

Please enclose a self-addressed stamped envelope for reply, or $1.00 to cover costs. If outside the USA, enclose an international postal reply coupon.

Many people have made this book possible, and I would like to give them a special thank you: Alan Wiley for his editorial help, and also for encouraging me to keep going when I lost faith in my ability to write; my loving kids for their hugs, kisses, constant encouragement, and patience; and my friends and family, who are always loved. Thank you!

FIRST EDITION
First Printing, 2014

Book design by Bob Gaul
Cover design by Gavin Duffy
Cover image: iStockphoto.com/15812486/EricVega
Editing by Ed Day

Llewellyn Publications is a registered trademark of Llewellyn Worldwide Ltd.

Library of Congress Cataloging-in-Publication Data (On file)
ISBN 978-0-7387-3926-7

Llewellyn Publications
A Division of Llewellyn Worldwide Ltd.
2143 Wooddale Drive
Woodbury, MN 55125-2989
www.llewellyn.com

Printed in the United States of America

Contents

Preface

Forgotten Burial is much more than a ghost story, it's a spiritual journey of discovery. I moved to an apartment in Chico, California, in the year 2000. Never in my wildest dreams would I have imagined the terror and confusion I was about to experience: lights flashing, the hands of the clock turning, and my three-year-old daughter's toy, a "Sing and Snore Ernie" doll, mysteriously relocated in the center of my living room, screaming, "I feel great! I feel great! I feel great!"...And this was just the first night I moved in. The strange anomalies continued. This paranormal adventure introduced me to the ghost of a missing college student; a notorious criminal by the name of Cameron Hooker; and his wife, Janice. In 1984, Cameron and Janice were linked to a story that made national headlines: "The Seven-Year Sex Slave."

Hooker and his wife seemed like typical young new-lyweds, according to the neighbors. However, they shared a secret: a desire for sadomasochism, torture, and violent pornography. Unfortunately, their own sick relationship wasn't enough. They wanted a sex slave; hence, a grand scheme evolved.

On January 31, 1976, the couple set out from their home in Red Bluff, California, on a mission. They soon found themselves in Chico, thirty-five miles south. Their horrible vision was about to become a reality.

The day was dark and dreary, and rain clouds were filling the sky when the pair spotted their victim walking alone down a neighborhood street lined with small family homes and neatly kept yards. She was beautiful, young, and thin—a Caucasian woman with long, brown hair. The afternoon was turning quickly to dusk. The colder winter weather yielded the perfect opportunity to stop and ask the girl if she needed a ride.

The couple pulled their light-blue Dodge Colt up next to her. The young woman on the sidewalk explained she had just left a flea market after an argument with her boyfriend. Right away, Cameron and Janice knew they had found their perfect victim.

The following week, a local newspaper, the *Enterprise-Record*, ran a picture and missing-persons report which read, "City police are asking for help in locating a missing teen. She was last seen January 31 and hasn't been seen since. She did not make it back to her apartment. Anyone with possible information is asked to come forward."

Soon weeks turned into months, months turned into years, and years turned into decades. The disappearance of the young woman remained an unsolved mystery—until my daughter and I moved into the last known residence of the missing girl. Through ghostly encounters, vivid dreams, and divine intervention, clues would soon be revealed.

My daughter, my friends, the residents of our town, and I were all affected by this mystery. My reality-bending adventures inspired me to write this compelling story.

Conversations have been reconstructed to the best of my memory, and some names have been changed to protect privacy. This book is composed of the opinions of the author and any allegations made about crimes possibly committed by Janice and Cameron Hooker are not intended as fact, but as the opinion of the author.

This book is dedicated to the victim's family.

ONE

Mysterious Abilities

I am not a professional psychic, but I am someone who has special abilities. I repressed these abilities for many years, that is, until I encountered a supernatural anomaly that reawakened my belief in the afterlife and completely changed my life.

I was born in 1967 to what some would consider a nonconformist mother. My two younger siblings and I had an unconventional life in the remote mountains of Berry Creek, California. My family lived off the land next to a Native American cemetery. I was homeschooled, rode horses, and took baths in nearby Lake Oroville. I was a sensitive child who experienced premonitions, intuition, extreme empathy, and what I later understood to be paranormal activity. When I was younger, I thought everyone's experience was similar—that they were like me.

My mother was born in 1948. As an only child, she was spoiled and rebellious. Her idol and role model growing up was John Wayne. As an adult she wore flannel shirts, blue jeans, and black cowboy boots. She rode, trained, and sold horses; smoked two packs of cigarettes a day, and had a couple of shots of whiskey each night to fall asleep. Aside from her long brown hair, worn in a braid, you might think she was a man.

After my mom went off to "rebel against the Man" in the late sixties, my brother Carl, sister Michelle, and I were mostly raised by my grandparents in a small mountain cabin with two rooms and a wood stove for heat. My father was absent most of my life because he traveled three weeks out of each month for his job as an engineer for the railroad. It was my grandfather, a retired mortician from Albany, New York, who shared spiritual ideas with me: ideas of acceptance, love, grief, and the possibility that life continued even after death. His philosophies on Christianity and Native American spirituality laid the foundation for my spiritual beliefs.

As a young child, I recall him saying in a distinctive New York accent, "Jodi, God puts signs, symbols, and spiritual teachers along life's journey to direct you to truth and understanding. Look not with your eyes, but look with the knowingness in the pit of your stomach—that is where God really resides."

He also used to say, "There is more than one way to find God." These words certainly rang true for me much later in life when I questioned reality, religion, and my sanity.

As a child, I had experienced a handful of significant paranormal anomalies, one of which was heart-wrenching and bittersweet. My first experience with death was a Native American funeral procession.

I was eight years old. I recall it was twilight, and late September. I was standing looking out the opened front window of my grandparent's log cabin with my little sister. She was six at the time. We were gazing at the full moon and stars illuminating the night sky when, off in the distance, I heard what sounded like singing, drumming, and crying. As my younger sister and I stood there looking at the moon, the sounds seemed to be getting closer and louder. Apparently my grandparents both heard the sounds as well. My grandfather ran out to the front porch to see what was happening. My sister, grandma, and I followed behind him.

Within seconds I saw about twenty or more Native Americans wearing buckskin clothing and headdresses covered in feathers walking together towards our house. Some of them were beating their chests, flailing their arms, wailing, and chanting as they neared our house. I thought they were coming to our house, but instead the group turned and walked up the dirt road to the right of our cabin.

As they walked by us, I could see four of the Natives carrying something on what looked like a buckskin stretcher. They continued to sing, drum, and wail. An older

Native American lady locked eyes with me. It was as if I could empathically feel all her pain. She continued to stare at me as she walked by with tears rolling down her cheeks, yet somehow she was also smiling. I didn't understand how I could feel what she was feeling.

My gaze turned from the old woman to the stretcher; lying there was an older, small-framed Native American man wrapped in some kind of tan cloth. I remember grabbing onto my grandpa's hand as I shook with fright and said, "What's going on, Grandpa? Who are those people? And what happened to the man?"

Grandpa picked me up and held me next to his chest and said, "Jodi, the Great Spirit came to take him home."

"Who is the Great Spirit, Grandpa? And where is the man's home?" I asked.

The procession of Natives continued walking up the hill, chanting and wailing in a language I didn't understand. Grandpa looked at me and said, "Christians know the Great Spirit as God, Jodi. The man has died and is going to heaven."

Since my grandfather was a mortician, he had respect and an open mind towards other cultures, and how people viewed death and spirituality.

My mom and dad were not around much when I was a child, but when they were, they would take my siblings and me to the mountain chapel for church with their hippie Jesus freak friends, so I did have some sense of heaven, God, Christianity, and the Holy Spirit.

That night, lying in my small twin bed with my little sister, listening to the far-off Native American death ritual being performed throughout the night, I couldn't help but think about death, God, what I had been taught by the Christian hippies. I also thought about the spiritual conversations I had with my grandfather, and a mysterious experience we'd shared earlier in the month.

My grandpa had worked many long, hard years in Orange County as a mortician, and upon his retirement decided to fulfill his childhood dream of living in the mountains. I remember Grandpa telling me that he and Grandma liked to gamble. One night he and Grams, as I called her, decided to get out a map and a pin. Grandpa spun a California map; and wherever Grandma stuck the pin would be where the family would move. It landed in the mountains of Berry Creek in northern California. He moved our family to Berry Creek in 1969.

My grandpa's joy in life was to take care of us kids, and trek my sister and me all over the mountains and creeks, encouraging us to explore. He especially liked taking us to his favorite turn-of-the-century dump sites next to the old pioneer cemetery ten miles north of our home.

A month earlier, during one of our outings, I remember walking up a small hill to a gray gravestone underneath a large pine tree, while my grandfather dug for turn-of-the-century treasures just outside of the cemetery. As I walked up and over the hill, I noticed a young lady in a long, pink, flowered dress and a light-colored bonnet. She was walking back and forth next to a grave. I decided to walk over to see if she was okay because she seemed worried. As I started to walk towards the woman, I heard my grandfather yell for me, so I turned around to see what he wanted.

He said, "Hey honey, did you see that lady in a long pink dress wearing a bonnet?"

I said, "She's right here!" But when I turned to look, she was gone, nowhere to be seen.

Grandpa stopped digging, and made his way up the hill and over to me. I remember him looking down at the gravestone where I had been standing with a perplexed expression. He said, "This is the gravestone of a baby who died in 1865."

I was shocked. This was the first time I had ever thought about a child dying. It seemed inconceivable to me, as an eight-year-old, that children died.

Grandpa looked at me and said, "The lady was probably the spirit of the baby's mother. Sometimes after people die, they check in to see how we are doing. Spirits and ghosts aren't scary like in the movies; they're actually people like you and me. In fact, someday you and I will be ghosts too."

As I lay there in the bed, covers over my head, listening to the Native American burial ritual being held on the mountaintop, I wondered if Grandpa might have been onto something. After all, he had been a mortician and a strongly spiritual man. He must have encountered many spiritual issues in his line of work.

January 31, 1976. I had my most life-altering paranormal experience yet. My mom and grandparents were planning a wonderful birthday party for me, and I knew that turning nine was going to be a magical event. I had been planning the day in my head for many months.

I had really wanted a mountain bike and had asked my grandfather for one. Secretly I knew my grandparents had gotten me one, and I was going to receive it on this magical occasion, along with a beautiful pair of gold earrings I had been admiring in the J.C. Penney catalog. My friends and family were all supposed to arrive around 2:00 p.m. I couldn't wait for the party to begin.

My mom had been traveling back and forth between Los Angeles and Berry Creek for a few years, hanging out with friends and a woman she called my godmother. Periodically Michelle, Carl, and I would travel with my mother and stay with her friend. My grandmother thought my mother needed to be more stable since she had just given birth to my brother Seth, her fourth child. So they moved us into a small trailer just a couple of miles up the road from them.

My birthday party was going to be momentous, and it would also be the first time we had entertained guests in our new place. I was so excited, I could barely contain myself. I thought it best that I wait for my friends and my grandpa outside. My grandmother worked as a secretary forty miles away in downtown Oroville, so she planned to come to the party after work.

I remember standing alone outside, waiting for my guests to arrive, next to a large, beautiful oak tree. As I waited, I saw my grandpa walking up the hill toward me with a giant smile on his face. He waved at me; I waved and smiled back. Then the strangest thing happened as he continued to walk toward me. His image started to fade. I blinked, and he vanished. I wondered where he had gone.

I decided to walk down the hill to see what had happened to him, but there was no Grandpa. I was confused. I ran farther down the road to see if I just missed him, but he wasn't there, so I walked back to my house to ask my mom where he was.

"Mom, I just saw Grandpa walking toward me, but I blinked my eyes and he was gone," I said.

"What do you mean, you blinked your eyes and he was gone?" Mom said. "Grandpa hasn't arrived yet."

"Mom, I am telling you the truth! I just watched Grandpa walk up the hill toward me a minute ago. He smiled and waved, and then, all of a sudden, he was gone."

My mom looked at me with concern in her eyes as though I was lying, and then said, "Stay here with the kids. I'll go look for him. Maybe his truck broke down."

Mom got into her Volkswagen van and drove down the hill to see if he was stranded on the side of the road somewhere. When she didn't find him or his truck, she decided to drive down to his house to see what was wrong, or what was keeping him.

When Mom arrived at his house, she found him lying on the couch. His heart had given out. His old dog, King, was next to him on the floor wailing, and his beloved cat, Charlie, was curled up on his chest.

On January 31, 1976, Grandpa Doug passed into God's great mystery. It was my ninth birthday.

The following week, my family and I took my grand-father's ashes up to the old pioneer cemetery, where we had seen the lady in pink. The family had a plaque made that read, "Grandpa Doug, our dear father, friend, rest in eternal peace." It was placed on a gigantic pine tree directly in front of the gravestone of the baby who died in 1865.

As our family stood there grieving, I thought to my-self; Grandpa actually made it to my birthday. He was just a ghost, like the lady in pink. I knew he would always watch over me, and never scare me like in the movies.

Shortly after my grandfather's passing, I was walking to school with my little sister, Michelle. There was nothing particularly different about this morning—just a cold win-ter day. I remember putting on my coat and boots. Being the big sister, I wanted to be the first out the front door.

As I walked down the road, I noticed an unfamiliar boy behind an old oak tree. He was looking at me and motioning with his hand to come to him. I looked back for my sister. She was about twenty yards behind.

I didn't recognize the boy. Looking closer, I noticed he didn't have a shirt on. He had brown skin and short, brown hair with bangs. He had something wrapped around his

waist. I thought, *this kid must be cold.* He was motioning for
to me to come to him. I was concerned because I knew we
were the only family on our road with kids. I was also confused about why he was dressed like a Native American.
In my child's mind, something was wrong, and he seemed
out of place.

I turned back to my sister and asked, "Who is that boy?"

"What boy?" she replied.

Her response scared me because he was standing about
ten feet in front of us. I didn't understand why she couldn't
see him and I could see him plain as day.

I whispered in her ear because I didn't want the boy
to hear me, and again I said, "Who is the boy?"

Again she said, "What boy?"

I looked at the Native American boy still standing in
front of me, motioning for me to come to him, and then
turned around, grabbed my sister's hand, and started to run
back home as fast as my little legs would go. I ran into our
house and into the back room where my mother was still
sleeping. I woke her up.

She could tell something was wrong by the look on
my face. "What's wrong?" she asked. "You and your sister
are supposed to be walking to your monthly homeschool
meeting at mountain chapel. Is everything okay?"

I was scared and confused and started to cry. I blurted
out, "There is an Indian boy out by the old tree. He was
just standing there alone, without a coat on. I think he
wanted to play. Michelle can't see him, but I can!"

"What do you mean, you can see him but Michelle can't?"

With a tears streaming down my face, I said, "Mom, please go see who it is. Something seems wrong."

Mom grabbed her coat and boots, and grumbled. "You woke me up because an invisible child doesn't have a coat on?" Within a few minutes, we headed out the door and down the dirt road. Unfortunately by the time we got to where the boy had been standing, he was gone. To me, what I had witnessed had seemed so real, and yet no one had seen the boy but me. Mom was mad because I had interrupted her sleep. She yelled at me, "You have an over-active imagination! Take your sister to your meeting, and don't wake me up unless there's a real emergency!"

At that moment I really wished my grandfather was there. I knew he would have understood. Later that day, my sister and I walked home from our school meeting, and as we passed the tree next to the creek, I held her hand tight, frightened that I might encounter him again. I don't know why I was scared, because he hadn't done anything; he had just seemed out of place.

After school that same day, my sister, brother, and I decided to take our horses for a ride. We used to ride our horses on the back road behind our house up on the old mountain. We would occasionally find interesting places to play. On this particular trip, we found a pretty clearing in the middle of the brush and pine trees. We got off the horses and started to look around. My brother immediately found an arrowhead on the ground by his feet; this prompted us to start looking around and dig in the dirt. To our surprise, we found many small beads, some crystals, and more arrowheads. Caught up in the fun, we continued for a couple of hours.

When darkness began to fall, I told my brother and sister it was time to go. We all put many small treasures, beads, and arrowheads into our pockets before we mounted the horses for the ride home.

That evening, when my mom came out to call us in for dinner, she happened to find us playing with all of the beads and arrowheads. She asked us where we had gotten them, and I told her. She started to yell at us, telling us to give her everything we had found.

"In the morning, you need to take me to where you found the artifacts," she said.

I didn't understand why, or what artifacts were.

"Mom, I am really sorry," I said. "We were just playing in a field with some plastic flowers, mounds of dirt, and rocks and we found all of this neat stuff and decided to bring it home." My mom wore a concerned look on her face as we sat and ate our dinner.

The next day, we rode the horses back to the location. As we came upon the spot, my mom looked startled. I asked her what was wrong. She said that this was a cemetery—a sacred place where the Native Americans from the mountains were buried. We needed to put the beads, crystals, and arrowheads back and say a prayer to the Native Americans, asking to be forgiven for disturbing their place of rest.

Michelle, Carl, and I sat and prayed, asking our Christian God and the Native Americans to forgive us. During the ride home, I realized the mysterious boy I had seen the day before had once lived on the mountain with his tribe. He had probably played—just like my brother, sister, and me—in the creeks and hills, with crystals and arrowheads. Maybe he was a ghost, or maybe I was a ghost to him. I didn't know or understand, and I was afraid to ask.

As a child, I didn't understand my ability to see spirit people. And since the only person in my life who understood these types of experiences had passed away, I didn't know where to turn. So I blocked my experiences with the spirit world far from my memory for many years.

After my grandfather's passing, my mother and father divorced, making this the first time Mom had to assume the parenting role. Unfortunately, she found motherhood a burden and preferred time alone, or with friends or other interests. My dad provided the basics—food, clothing, and a roof over our heads, but they were both disastrous on an emotional level. Sometimes out of sheer frustration, my mom would go into a rage and spank or slap us kids.

I was the oldest child, and since my grandmother worked forty miles away, mom had to lean on me physically and emotionally. It was fairly awful, and as a preteen and teen I started to suffer from severe bouts of anxiety.

One late night in 1979, I recall lying in my small twin bed next to my sister Michelle. I was sick to my stomach and nervous. I shook uncontrollably, and it was hard to breathe. Even though it was freezing cold, beads of sweat dripped from my forehead and down my cheeks; thoughts of the spirit world and my grandpa's death filled my mind. I tried to comfort myself by getting up to sit at the edge of my bed. Sitting up didn't seem to help, so I draped my orange comforter with bright green flowers over my head. Somehow, inside I felt like I wanted to run and hide at the same time, I felt detached from reality. I didn't know what was happening to me. I felt as though this frightening episode might be the end of my young twelve-year-old life.

I really wanted to run into my mom's bedroom to have her comfort me, to wrap her arms around me and tell me I was okay, and that I wasn't dying. But you see, my mom raised us kids that to show outward signs of fright, affection, or to shed a tear was a sign of weakness.

As I sat practically paralyzed with fear, I remember nudging my sister's foot to wake her as I sat quietly crying. Breathless, I said, "Michelle, something's wrong. I think I am dying."

"Shhhh," she said. "Hermie is sleeping in the other room, Jodi. Don't wake her up or she will come in here and yell or spank us."

Michelle got up from our bed and walked over to me, put her arm around me, and said, "You're okay, big sis, I won't let anything happen to you." She was only ten at the time. She could see I was really scared, so she walked over to our bedroom window, quietly opened it up, and said, "Jodi, come over here to get some fresh air."

I shakily walked over to the opened window, looked out and over towards the dirt road where the Native American funeral procession had taken place, and took in a deep breath. My mouth was dry, which made quietly swallowing my tears nearly impossible. I cried with my sister's arm around me. I waited for the frightful episode to pass, but it didn't, sadness and the desperation for my mother's touch overcame me. Choking back my tears, I said to my sister, "I need Hermie, I can't take this scariness. If I am dying, I want to be next to her." I knelt to the ground as I continued to shake and cry, and then started to slowly and softly crawl on my hands and knees, like a small frightened animal, out the bedroom and down the dark hallway to my mother's room. The crackling of the wood stove and hard wooden floor made each subtle movement seem extraordinarily loud. I looked back at my sister; she was now sitting at the end of the bed crying.

She wiped her sleepy wet eyes, and whispered, "Jodi I am scared. Please don't get in trouble."

I looked over at her as we both quietly wept and said, "Michelle, if I die tonight and become a ghost, remember I love you, and would never scare you."

I made my way into Hermie's room, and secretly slid underneath her bed. The tiny space was like a coffin, but I didn't care, the mere of sound of my mother's breath was comforting. I lay there waiting to die, softly weeping with tears rolling down my face. I remember in that moment, my mother's hand hung over the side of the bed. All I longed for was the reassurance that I was okay, so I dared to reach up and softly touch her pinky finger to mine. As I did, my heart regained its regular beat, and I knew that I was no longer going to die.

TWO

Gift from God

It was a sweltering summer day, about 105 degrees, June of 1980. I was thirteen. My sister and I decided to walk to the lake to take a swim. We were innocently walking in sandals and bikinis, half naked about a mile and half from our house. I recall the blazing sun hitting my face and shoulders, making me tired and causing me to perspire profusely. I remember saying to my sister: "Hey, Michelle, let's try and hitchhike to the lake; it's too hot to walk." Wiping the sweat off her brow she said, "Yeah, I think that is a good idea."

Within a few minutes we heard a car coming up the road. We stood next the road picking blackberries, drenched in sweat as a small light-colored car pulled up next to us. Something about the look of the car, however, prevented me from sticking my thumb out. In the driver's seat was a young man who looked to be in his twenties. He was wearing sunglasses, had red hair, pale skin with freckles, and appeared to be alone. He leaned his head out the window and with a strange smile on his face, said, "It sure is hot out today. You cute young ladies looking for a ride?" Though his words seemed innocent enough, it was his leering, and the strange smirk on his face that gave me a creepy feeling.

"No, thank you," I replied. "My sister and I are just on our way to the lake to take a swim and we feel like walking."

Michelle looked over at me confused and said, "I am really hot. Let's take the ride."

I looked at my sister and shook my head just so slightly to let her know that we didn't need a ride.

As we stood there a small breeze seemed to come out of nowhere kicking up the red dust, which created a swirl that resembled angel wings. This made me take notice of the feelings I had had in the pit of my stomach—it knew that we should not take a ride. The man said one again, "It's awfully hot out. Are you sure I can't give you a ride somewhere?"

"No, we are going to walk, but thank you," I replied. The man started to drive away slowly, but I could see him staring back at us through his rearview mirror. As soon as he drove out of sight around the corner, I yelled, "Run Michelle, run!" All I could see was the back of my sister's shoulder-length blond hair dancing in the wind as she darted around the blackberry bushes and into the cluster of thick Manzanita bushes nestled beneath the tall pine trees.

Something was wrong. I could hear the sound of the small compact car revving its motor, screech at the corner, and start back down the road towards us. "I'm right behind you. Go, go!" I yelled. "Don't look back. Just keep going, up and into the brush!" My heart beat fast, my head was spinning, and I felt like I was going to die. I ran as fast as I could behind my sister.

"Jodi, who was that weird man?" Michelle said quietly, as we sat hidden in the bushes peering out towards him. He had stopped his car and was now standing on the side of the road looking for us.

"He seemed really weird," said Michelle.

"Oh my God, I know, something about that man scares me, he looks like he could be one of those crazy religious people," I replied. We watched him for a minute. When he didn't find us, he got into his car and drove off. I had a feeling my sister and I narrowly escaped our demise.

As a teenager in the late 1970s, I lived an hour from the closest town, and since my mother wasn't around to take us anywhere, she encouraged us to hitchhike. We met some interesting people, mostly hippies or older folks or friends from the hill. I have to admit after that horrifying hitchhiking experience with my sister, I seriously wondered just how many teenage girls met their end hitchhiking, and why they didn't listen to the knowingness in the pit of their stomach when something seemed wrong.

During the mid- and late 1970s, not only was hitch-hiking encouraged, but so was exploration of religious freedom. The postwar generation of the sixties and seventies wanted to change the world, unfortunately many kids suffered because young parents wanted to rebel against the Man. Considering that there were a lot of crazy religious groups that called themselves Christians, it's no wonder some people were confused, misled, and self-indulgent.

In 1977, I became aware of some of these alternative religious groups. One group called the Children of God was rumored to be having sex with children. Then there was the Peoples Temple, known for the largest mass suicide in history, taking out mostly children and young adults, all in the name of God. As I grew older, so did my awareness of life and the world around me.

One night at the age of fifteen, two of my friends came over to visit me. They had just bought a '72 Volkswagen Bug. We all hung out talking and listening to music, when all of a sudden I had a vision in my mind's eye. I saw my friends driving home, and crashing their car into a mountainside. I didn't know what to say or do.

After sitting and visiting for a while I looked over at my friend and said, "Hey, Russ, on your way home tonight, drive really carefully, I have a strange feeling that something bad might happen." He looked at me and said, "Jodi, you're such a weirdo. We always drive safely." That night on the way home, my friends crashed into the side of the mountain.

I was convinced that I might have had something to do with it. I didn't want to be like one of these crazy religious freaks who followed Jim Jones or the Children of God. I wondered if I was evil, possessed, or crazy.

When I was sixteen, I had intermittent premonitions, mostly small things such as thinking of someone, and then having them call or show up. It seemed that, for the most part, my strange abilities diminished. Unfortunately, the panic attacks increased and seemed to have me in their grip. My mother couldn't stand the fact that I was showing signs of weakness and was basically pissed off because these panic attacks were interfering with her ability to be a non-parent.

One night I was having trouble breathing and felt like I needed to cry. I didn't want my mother to catch me crying, so I went outside and sat on our front porch to quietly calm myself. I was staring up at the full moon when suddenly I heard the front door start to open; I wiped the tears from my eyes and turned to see who was coming. It was my mom. She had a stunned look on her face, and a paper in her hand. She walked towards me, stood over me, and said, "Jodi, I have had just about enough of your crying jags and strange temper tantrums!"

The howling of wind whipped though the pine trees, creating an eerie echo of my mother's strong, resounding voice. I looked up at my mom, choking back tears. "Mom, I am sorry. I can't help feeling emotions so deeply. Sometimes I have to cry, which makes it hard to breathe."

"Jodi, showing outward signs of emotion is not acceptable in this family!"

She leaned over and handed me the paper. "Read this, and give me your answer in three days!"

The wind continued to howl as the pine trees swayed in the wind. Mom turned around and walked back into the house. I held the note in my hand, the full moon creating just enough light for me see and began to read. Written with a bold black marker:

Dear Jodi:

These attacks are interfering with your babysitting responsibilities and chorus. You need to get yourself together and stop this emotional weakness. I love you because I had you, but I don't like your personality, I wanted to create strong, unemotional kids. Children that are self reliant, and that work hard; we have 50 horses that need tending to. I need to be able to count on you, so I can leave when I want or need to. I don't want the other kids to learn from your emotional example so, if you are not able to get your emotions under control, then it is your responsibility to find other living arrangements!

I couldn't believe what I was reading. I was only sixteen. I started to shake and tremble with fright. I looked up at the illuminated night sky and prayed:

"Dear God, I am scared, I don't know what to do. Where or who should I turn to?" Right then, an answer came to me. I stopped crying. A wave of calmness and peace ran through me. I walked into the house, picked up the phone, and called someone I hadn't seen, nor talked to in a few years; my godmother, Debbie.

———

Debbie had five kids, three older than me and two younger. She was one of my mother's Christian, Jesus freak friends from Orange County, California. Debbie was in her forties, married, went to church regularly, and had a more traditional lifestyle. I always enjoyed the time we spent with Debbie's family, and remember her saying to me when I was younger, "Jodi, if you ever need a place to come to, you're welcome here."

With the precision of a surgeon, my mother grabbed the phone from my hand and started making arrangements for me to move in with Debbie. Within three days, Mom shipped me away off to my new family, seemingly without a single emotion. My unconventional life in the mountains for the past sixteen years was now a thing of the past.

For the next three years, I lived with my godmother and her family. I was introduced to Sunday school, Wednesday worship services, and a whole new group of friends. I was indoctrinated with black and white Christian values, taught about sin, and how other ways of thinking and knowing things were from the devil.

These new Christian values contradicted what my grandpa had taught me. But I didn't care—I wanted to forget about my past, the anxiety, premonitions, and ghostly encounters. I was a good Christian now, living with a new stable family, and I didn't want to do or say anything that would jeopardize my living situation. I didn't ever want to feel abandoned again. So I prayed for God to take away whatever strange abilities I had and to give me a new life, forgiven of sin and devilish ways.

God did what I asked, and for the next few years, life seemed to be, for the most part, what most Christian Americans would consider normal. I went to school, graduated, and worked as a medical assistant. I dated, lived with roommates, and was comfortably numb—for the most part, happy.

I rarely talked to my biological family, and over the years we all kind of went our separate ways. My mom had moved away to Montana, and my siblings were scattered all over the western United States. My grandma remained in Berry Creek, and I remained in Orange County, California.

As I got older, I longed to have a family of my own someday, but having a child seemed out of reach. By the time I was twenty-nine, I had been told by two doctors that due to a medical condition, getting pregnant would be next to impossible. I was devastated, but eventually came to terms with my infertility. Yet I secretly prayed each night that someday I might be lucky enough to get married and have my own child.

After my grandpa's passing in the mid-seventies, my grandmother, whom I called "Grams," had been living by herself. She was feisty, and extremely independent. But at the age of eighty-three, her independence was interrupted by a cancer diagnosis. Though we had been apart for a few years, in my soul I knew I needed to take care of her. Since I was a medical assistant, I decided to move back to Berry Creek. I somehow thought she was invincible and would recover from cancer, but unfortunately, her health continued to decline and we needed to move from the mountain and closer to town to be near her doctors. We moved to Chico, California, in 1996.

The year wasn't all sickness and pain. We spent many fun times together in Chico. One of our special treats together was going to the neighborhood diner for breakfast and then for walks in Bidwell Park.

On my thirtieth birthday, Grams became extremely sick. She had taken a turn for the worse and ended up in the hospital. I feared this would be her last day with me. But to my agony and surprise, she hung in there a few more days; maybe it was because she didn't want my birthday to hold another tragedy for me. She passed on the morning of February 7, 1997.

I held her hand when she took her last breath, and the last thing I said to her before she passed into God's great mystery was, "Grams, I love you so much. I will miss you.

When you see God, tell him I want to have a baby." She smiled at me for a brief moment, and then her spirit left her body. She had been there when I came into this world and took my first breath, and I was there as she took her last breath and left this world. The moment was bittersweet.

The night my grandmother passed, my ex-boyfriend, Ryan, whom I hadn't seen for a year, heard about my grandmother's passing. He decided to come over to express his condolences and to comfort me. I remember him holding me tightly in his arms as we grieved the loss of my dear grandma. We reminisced about great times we'd spent together with Grams and agreed that now she would be my guardian and protector.

One night shortly after Grams's passing, I had an amazing dream. In it, my grandmother came to me dressed in a brilliant gold outfit. She sat next to me on my bed, lovingly watching me with a huge smile.

She reached over and held my hand, looked me in the eyes, and said, "Jodi, you are going to have a baby. Her name will be Hannah Rose."

I was so excited to be with Grams once again. "Grams, I've missed you; please stay with me," I said.

"I am always with you, and you will know when you look into your new baby's eyes," she replied. "Now rest, and I will see you in your dreams."

When I woke up, I thought about how real the dream had seemed. I was thankful to have seen Grams once again. I woke up Ryan, who was sleeping next to me, to tell him about the extremely vivid dream. We had rekindled our romance. Ryan, being a spiritual person and part Native American, expressed his thoughts and beliefs about the afterlife and the dreams.

"I believe in ghosts and in Native American ways," he said. "I believe our spirits have the opportunity to visit people and places to share messages before passing on to God. Most of the time these visits are during our dreams." His family was part of the Wintu tribe from Mount Shasta, located in Northern California.

Interesting, I thought, this was the first time since childhood that I had had a conversation with anyone regarding a spiritual belief other than Christianity.

"What do you mean?"

"I was taught that after people die, our spirits have a chance to visit relatives and friends," Ryan explained. "Our spirits have the opportunity to address unresolved issues, and can also help in other ways unknown to the living."

A flood of hidden memories reawakened inside of me. I didn't realize just how profound the dream and conversation I had shared with Ryan that morning would become.

Three weeks had passed since Grams appeared in my dream. I was feeling sick and thought I had the flu and depression after my great loss. However, as the days went on, my health failed to improve, and I decided to call my doctor. Although he suggested my symptoms were correlated with depression, he wanted to schedule a complete examination.

As I hung up the phone, I sat down on the end of my bed, took a deep breath, and let out a sigh of sadness…but as I did, the dream and the conversation with Ryan came to mind. I started to laugh—and then scream with joy. I realized that, as Ryan had suggested, my Grams had come to visit. She was a messenger from God. I wasn't sick, I was pregnant! I was so excited that I rushed to the pharmacy and bought five pregnancy tests. Back at home, I ran to the bathroom and ripped open the tests. Lo and behold, each test gave a positive result! One even had a smiling face staring back at me! I was laughing so hard I fell to my knees. I imagined Grams immediately arriving in heaven and telling God how her granddaughter needed a baby.

Through laughter and tears, I called my doctor to update him with the good news. He set up a different type of appointment for the following week.

At the doctor's office, as I lay on the sterile table waiting for the test results, my thoughts settled on my grandma and the conversation with Ryan. After what seemed like an eternity, the nurse finally came in and said, "It looks as if you're now about five weeks pregnant."

It was now a reality; I was pregnant. The news was validation that the visit from my grandma was real. Although it went against my Christian upbringing, just like both Ryan and my grandfather had shared, it now seemed possible that a spirit could communicate even after death.

The nurse noticed the strange, contemplative look on my face, and said, "Miss Foster, are you okay?"

I took a deep breath. "Oh, I am fine, ma'am."

She just smiled at me as though I were just another hormonally insane woman and then said, "It looks as though your conception date was February seventh."

I knew she was right, because the only time Ryan and I were intimate was February seventh.

I started to cry and said to the nurse, "February seventh was the day my Grams passed over!"

At the end of my ultrasound, I hugged the nurse and said, "Thank you! Thank you!"

She laughed at me, and as she turned to walk out of the room and said, "You're welcome sweetie, and congratulations!"

I knew that my sweet child was on her way. As the weeks passed, I contemplated the dream and the significance of the name Hannah Rose. I went to the local library and looked for a book on baby names. I found out that Hannah means "gift from God." I started to cry as chills ran down my spine.

My pregnancy was long and difficult. I went into labor on Halloween 1997. I thought my angel was going to be born around midnight; however, she waited, and on November 1, 1997, I delivered a beautiful baby girl. The first of November is the Day of the Dead, a holiday celebrated around the world in honor of ancestors and saints who have passed on—another reminder to me of the spiritual realm and the continuation of life after death. Ryan and I named our child Hannah Rose.

THREE

Leaving Montana

After Hannah's birth, I had heard through a mutual friend that my sister Michelle missed me and wanted to talk. I was nervous about connecting with her because it had been a few years since we had last talked. Ryan had started to use drugs and ended up going to jail. I was really lonely, missed my grandma, and had a small child, so I took a chance on a phone call that ended with an invitation to move to Montana.

Two weeks later, I sold everything I had, and Hannah and I moved to Eureka, Montana. We lived next to my mother's tepee, in a warm Amish log cabin. Unfortunately, Montana was not what I expected. It was about ten degrees below zero, with at least five feet of snow on the ground, and I was recovering from the flu. Hermie, an avid hunter and survivalist, was now a hard-core alcoholic and on another of her drinking binges. She paced around the cabin with a rifle in her hand, verbally assaulting my character while she was shaking physically. Years of pent-up tension and anger, short-circuited by the mental displacement of alcohol, preceded this unrestrained release.

I recall Hermie lifting a rifle and pointing it in my direction. What I saw in her eyes looking down the barrel of that gun made me frightened for my life, and for that of my child, Hannah. All I could do was grab my daughter and run out the front door, screaming, "Mom! Please don't hurt us! Please! Don't!"

My legs felt as if they were going to give out underneath me as I ran outside to the only escape I had—a blue Chevy Blazer. I remember looking up to the dark night sky as I ran, wondering *What am I going to do now?* This was rural Montana, in the far north, near the Canadian border, and the neighbors were few and far between.

The last few hours with my mother had been emotionally and physically draining.

My body was weak from the flu and anxiety, and my only option was to jump into the Blazer, put it in four-wheel drive, and head down the dark, winding, snow-ridden road. I felt lost, sick, and alone; confusion and fear were my companions. Not only did icy roads lurk beneath the freshly fallen snow, but I started to suffer from agoraphobia and panic attacks—and at times, just leaving my home and driving in general made me extremely panicked. But the only way for Hannah and me to be safe was to get out from under the wrath of my mother, so with tears in my eyes and a lump in my throat, I drove, searching for the nearest place I could get help and rest.

After about an hour of driving, I found myself at a combination gas station and motel called the Huckleberry Inn, a popular stop for truck drivers and travelers on their way into the Canadian mountains.

I remember how extremely scared and alone I felt as I pulled in. Having only lived in Montana a short time, I did not know anyone. I sat for twenty minutes in the snow-filled parking lot, crying and trying to catch my breath, before getting out of my warm Blazer. With Hannah bundled next to me, hugging my hips, I made my way over to the motel's front door.

Walking in to the building that had once been a log cabin, I caught my reflection in a mirror hanging behind the long, wooden counter: I looked as white as a ghost and was wearing the same nightgown I had worn for the past three days. The motel attendant, a robust woman with red hair worn in a bun, looked startled. I know she noticed my disheveled appearance and could tell that something was quite wrong.

After we stared at each other in silence for what seemed to be an eternity, she asked, "Can I help you?"

Breathless and unable to hold back my tears, I managed to say, "I only have three hundred dollars to my name, and I need a place to stay." The moment was uncomfortable.

Thank heaven above, the woman showed an uncommon kindness, changing my run of bad luck. She offered to rent me a warm, safe, cozy room for a week for only one hundred dollars. As Hannah and I walked over to our new sanctuary, snowflakes fell, creating a pattern in the night sky that reminded me I wasn't alone; I had a higher power guiding my steps.

I recall letting out a sigh of relief. However, I knew my journey had just begun.

I spent the next week in the warm motel trying to regroup. I never expected that I would be a single mother, alone in rural Montana. I had little money and no friends, and now my mother's condition had made it impossible to live with her. I needed a plan.

To my great surprise, the motel attendant came to me on our last night and told me about a tiny cabin for rent just down the road. I recall her saying, "The cabin is old and dingy, twelve-by-twelve feet, with a wood stove. It might be what you need until you can figure things out." She then said kindly, "There is also a food bank two miles down the road if you're in need of assistance."

Though her intentions were kind and her heart was in the right place, I was embarrassed. Reality set in: I was alone, scared, and unsure of my future. I was low on money and gas. If I was going to survive, I had better accept the gracious offer and take all the help I could get. Her thoughtfulness was a gentle reminder that a higher power was looking out for Hannah and me.

The following morning, I gathered my things, bundled Hannah up in her warm yellow baby gear, and readied myself for our new adventure.

During those long, cold winter nights in our tiny log cabin, I slept with Hannah, bundled next to the fire, dreaming about the kind of life I wanted to give my daughter. Hannah was a gift from God, and I wanted to give her a good life. I had not chosen single motherhood, but through unfortunate circumstances, I now had to make do.

I found myself thinking back on fond memories, good times, and friends in Chico. I longed for the California sun, bike riding in Bidwell Park, and the wonderful cultural events Chico offered. Eureka was beautiful, but it was hard living for a poor single mother. Something about the little college town called me back. I could feel it deep in my soul.

———

Hannah and I continued to live in Montana in the small cabin, and I volunteered at the food bank. I made do with what I had, but I was anxious to change my circumstances.

One day after I had moved into the cabin, an older gentleman with graying hair and a scruffy beard came knocking on my door. He was the cabin's owner and had heard through the grapevine that I might need a job. He wanted to renovate the old hospital directly behind the cabin and turn it into a historic museum. First, he needed people to go into the building and remove stored items and equipment left from years gone by. I really needed the money, so I agreed to check out the work. I walked with him over to the hospital to take a look around.

When I walked in, what I saw was cold, dark, and gruesome. Cobwebs surrounded what looked to be old, long-forgotten hospital equipment lying around. It looked like a deranged surgeon's laboratory from a horror movie. As I walked through the abandoned hospital, I felt the hair on the back of my neck and arms stand on end. There was an uneasy presence in the room, but I couldn't see it. I only felt it. And I felt it in the pit of my stomach. I wondered if the place might be haunted; however, I wasn't sure at the time what "haunted" meant. Somehow I equated haunted with the negative feelings and the strange energy I was experiencing. All I knew was that I felt uneasy, and didn't want to spend much time there, especially alone. Unfortunately, I needed the money, so I agreed to help him the next day.

The following morning, I headed to work. I was relieved to see he had hired others; mostly young Montana boys who lived in town, drank a lot of beer, and liked to hunt for elk. While working, everyone talked, getting to know one another. We talked about the town's history and where we were all from. I was one of only two women working the job. The guys paid us a lot of attention.

The old hospital was a hard place for me to be. The antique equipment, musty smell, and macabre environment stirred in me feelings I could not explain. Other than the experience when my grandmother came to visit me in a dream, I pretty much denied my abilities and memories and tried to suppress them, due to my Christian mind-set. Somehow no matter how hard I tried to deny my feelings, I was aware of otherworldly spirits in the room. It was as though I could sense death, oppression, and a strange heaviness in the cold air. I prayed, "Please God, all I want to do is make some money. I don't want to feel scared while doing so. Please take these feelings away." And God did what I asked.

While working, I met a man nine years younger than me. He was tall and dark, with beautiful blue eyes. I could tell he was a kind man. His name was Brian. I told him I was freaked out by the old hospital, and that I didn't like to go in alone. Of course, he saw me as a damsel in distress and shadowed me as I went in and out.

He was cute, nice, and helpful. He even carried Hannah on his back so I could have a break for a while. The work was hard and the days were long and cold. I looked forward to the day's end, when I could escape the eerie old hospital for the warmth of my cabin.

After I finished work for the day, I said goodbye to my new friends. And as I walked away, Brian said, "I was wondering if you could use some company tonight. Are you hungry? If you are, I would love to cook dinner for you."

I couldn't resist his blue eyes and sexy smile. I said, "If you're not too tired, I would really enjoy that."

The food and conversation were good. He shared how he had moved from Oregon to Montana with his mother, brother, and stepfather a couple of years earlier.

He was interesting, and looking at a hot Montana boy was just the kind of fun I needed. For the first time in a while, I felt safe and peaceful knowing there was someone next to me.

Brian and I started to casually date, and as the week passed, my new friend and I kept working to restore the hospital. It was hard, but the pay was worth it. I knew once I had enough money saved, options for the future would open up.

While I worked, I often thought about moving back to Chico. I missed the warm sun and old friends. One evening, while sitting in the little cabin with Hannah, I started to feel really sad and lonely. I decided to drive to a pay phone to call my good friend Jenny, who lived in Chico. It had been a long time since we had talked, and I really missed her. During our conversation, I cried, revealing the struggles I had endured and the terrible predicament I was in.

Jenny, always a problem solver, said, "Why don't you sell your Blazer? That, along with the money you're earning, will give you enough to move back."

It hadn't occurred to me that selling my Blazer was an option. "That's a great idea—then I would have enough money to rent a place once I got to Chico."

We talked for a couple hours, reminiscing and making plans. In my soul, I knew Chico was where I wanted to raise

Hannah. Jenny extended an invitation to stay with her until I found my own place. When I hung up, I felt a sense of peace, knowing that it was only a matter of time before I could move. Time seemed to pass slowly during those long days working on the old hospital. Snow fell continually, and the ice thickened. Though I felt at constant odds with the weather, my cabin was a little sanctuary. My new friend Brian kept me stocked up with firewood, and after his hunting sessions, he would bring Hannah and me elk or deer meat. I was pretty good at making dinner on the wood stove, so Brian would stop by often.

Even though Brian's company was great, I still longed for a warmer climate. One night, while we were lying next to the fire chatting, I told him I was thinking about moving back to California. He said maybe he could convince me to stay. Most women would kill to have this kind of fantasy, but despite Brian's ploys to keep me around—and trust me, he made it hard to leave—I remained determined to move.

FOUR

What a Long, Strange Trip It's Been

It was now September 9, 1999. I had saved enough money to move. Throughout the months, I had continued talking to my good friend Jenny. We had laid the foundation for my move back home to Chico. The only obstacle now was that I continued to suffer from severe panic attacks and agoraphobia. Traveling was one of my biggest struggles.

It occurred to me that having a traveling companion who knew how to handle a person with panic attacks would help me to get home and feel safe while doing so. I called a hospital in nearby White Fish and asked if they would put a "help wanted" sign up for me that read, "Traveling companion for mom with panic attacks." I got a call from a nice male nurse who had family in Chico that he was going to visit. He told me he was a Christian man, and that he understood my condition since his sister also suffered from panic attacks. I knew this was a sign from God. Soon Hannah and I would be on our way.

It was hard to leave the new friends and kind strangers who had helped me while I was living in the cold mountains of Montana. Neither my mom nor my sister were in contact with me. This was the second time my mom had abandoned me—only this time I had a child, and nowhere to turn. Thank God for the help and kindness of others, because if it wasn't for them, Hannah and I might not have survived the cold.

Our journey to Chico began as I boarded a train with Hannah in the small town of Whitefish, Montana, looking forward to our new lives together, blessed by the experience of knowing the kindness of Montana, and eager to know Chico once again. We made our journey together on the Starlight Express, a beautiful train that travels the West Coast through Montana, Washington, Oregon, and then, finally, California. I spent the wonderful trip holding Hannah on my lap, and watching the wonders of each town and the beautiful landscape drift by.

Excitement and anxiety ran through my bones with each passing mile. Images of my future life with Hannah in Chico played over and over in my mind. As our trip neared its end I suffered a panic attack. We were going through the town of Red Bluff, California, just forty-five miles north of Chico. I felt a sense of impending doom and dread; my throat felt tight, and it was hard to breathe. I wasn't sure why. My traveling companion sitting next to me asked, "Are you okay?"

I replied, "What a long, strange trip these past few months have been."

He patted me on the back, and said, "You're almost home, friend. With all the hard work, planning, and anticipation, a slight amount of anxiety and panic seems only natural." I looked out the window at the town of Red Bluff whizzing by, took a deep breath and said, "You're probably right; it's all the anticipation and excitement." Strangely the hairs on the back of my neck and my arms stood on end, and I didn't really believe my own statement.

Twenty minutes out of Red Bluff, I could smell agriculture and could see the many olive, almond, and walnut trees Chico was known for. I remembered the voice of the conductor announcing, "Next stop: Chico." My heart and mind started to race with joy. Finally, we were home.

The train stopped. We got off and stepped down onto the hot pavement. All of a sudden, I was reminded of just how hot Chico really was. But even with the heat blasting me in the face, I was still filled with joy and gratefulness and a thankful heart. We had made it! We had finally made it back to Chico, California. After I thanked my traveling companion for his time and comfort, we hugged and went our separate ways. I walked over to a pay phone in the train station and called for a taxi. The taxi drove Hannah and me over to Jenny's house. She welcomed us with open arms, smiles, and a wonderful home-cooked meal. Jenny had invited me to stay with her for as long as I needed. However, after a couple of weeks, it was time I got out of her hair and found a place of my own.

I had saved enough money to live comfortably for about six months, and I had sold my Blazer before leaving Montana so I would have a deposit—first and last month's rent—when I finally found a place. After some searching, I came across an affordable apartment. I talked to the manager, whose name was Kelly. We talked for a while, and I told her about my struggle to get back home to Chico and how I wanted to start a new life with my daughter.

"I think we have exactly the kind of environment, and price, you are looking for," Kelly said.

"I am looking for a downstairs apartment if you have one," I replied, "since Hannah is little, and the thought of her falling down the stairs scares me."

Unfortunately, the only apartment she had open at the time was upstairs.

"Would you take the upstairs apartment for now?" Kelly asked. "We will have a downstairs apartment coming up soon."

"Yes, I would. And as soon as the downstairs unit becomes available, please let me know."

The following week, I moved into my new upstairs apartment with the help of Jenny and some other friends. I didn't have much other than the two suitcases Hannah and I had traveled with and a few things that friends had given to me, but it didn't matter to me; I was finally in Chico. I felt a sense of comfort and achievement.

Little did I know that my soul journey had just begun! I thought living in the harsh cold Montana snow was hard. Not even in my wildest dreams could I have imagined the life-altering supernatural experience that was in store for me in my new apartment.

FIVE

Haunting Nightmares

Hannah and I set up house in our new apartment. It was quaint; the neighbors were mostly college kids and a few older folks. One day, while walking around the complex with Hannah, I met a nice man in his sixties named Fred. Fred had lived in the complex since the early 1970s. According to him, it had been quite modern and stylish when it was first built, but thirty years later, it was a little run-down. A nice pool lay at the center of the complex, with a rose garden surrounding it and beautiful large oak trees, which provided a good amount of shade. While it wasn't the upscale complex it used to be, I was happy to be there after living in a cold, twelve-by-twelve Montana cabin.

After a couple weeks passed, I was finally settled in and was looking forward to getting out and around with Hannah.

One of my favorite places in Chico was One-Mile swimming hole in Bidwell Park. The entire park was nearly eleven miles long—one of the twenty-five largest in the United States. One of its long-lasting claims to fame is its association with the original Hollywood movie *The Adventures of Robin Hood,* starring Errol Flynn, which was filmed there in 1938, among the majestic oak and sycamore trees. Grams and I had taken walks there before she died, and I couldn't wait to take Hannah.

One morning, I decided to take Hannah on a bike ride to show her the wonderful park. It was as beautiful as I remembered. Sitting among the beautiful trees, I took a deep breath and thought about how I had once walked hand in hand with my grandmother, and now here I was walking hand in hand with my gift from God, Hannah. I felt blessed. Chico was starting to feel like home.

Nights at the new apartment were quiet. I didn't have a television or stereo, so I would lie in bed reading the Bible or self-help books, searching for comfort and answers regarding the experiences I had as a child, and now as an adult. The feelings I experienced in the old Montana hospital and the visit from Grams after her death were things I couldn't explain as a rational adult. It was beyond my understanding. Grandpa and Ryan both believed that life continued even after death, but my Christian upbringing conflicted with their theory.

One night I remember laying in bed thinking about God, mysteries, religion, and what prompted my decision to become a Christian.

It was the mid-1970s, and there was a hippie, groovy Jesus movement happening in the alternative subculture that my mother was a part of. I recall being in a 1972 Volkswagen van, driving down an old winding dirt road with my mother and three siblings.

We had just attended a mountain revival meeting and were on our way home. My little nine-year-old mind was racing and my little body trembled with excitement after the charismatic meeting. The pastor had talked about this wonderful man known as Jesus, a person sent to Earth by God to forgive me of my sins, a man created in the image of God who was actually God's son ... sent on his behalf to love me and accept me no matter what. Wow, to me this sounded like a get-out-of-hell-free card ...!

I remember looking out the van window at the trees whizzing by. As it started to get dark, I could still see glimpses of Lake Oroville to my left. I recall the sun just starting to set over the dam as I looked up from the VW bench seat over at my mother in the driver's seat and said, "Hermie, what do I need to do to have Jesus be my savior? I was thinking about what the preacher had said, and well, I really don't want to go to hell. So, I think I would like to have Jesus in my heart to be my savior."

Hermie looked into the rearview mirror at me for a second, then continued to look ahead at the curvy, bumpy road in case a deer darted out in front of us, and said, "It's simple. Just ask Jesus to be your Lord and Savior. Then ask him to forgive you of all your sins."

I closed my tiny eyes tightly and thought about my tainted nine-year-old past. I had kicked my sister earlier. I had yelled at my brother and called him a fart head. Hmmm, what else had I said or done that needed forgiveness?

"Jesus," I said under my breath, "Please be my Lord and Savior…uhhh, oh and please forgive me for my sins. Love you, and I guess that is it for now, sir."

As I opened my eyes I somehow thought I was going to see an angel or a burning bush, maybe the "Star-Spangled Banner" would miraculously play, or possibly the Lord himself would appear in the sky over the dam to welcome me into this new Christian world. But no, all that happened was that I felt a weight lifted off my young, sin-filled shoulders.

I was now saved, and just like the preacher said, I was now assured of my place in the afterlife. Whew, I thought to myself as an adolescent, "Whooo ha! Disaster and the devil's den were now averted!"

My Christian leaders and spiritual mentors explained life's existence, mysteries, and spirituality in very black-and-white, absolute terms. I was taught that angels and demons exist. Angels were created beings, nonhuman spirits created for the sole purpose of serving and carrying out the will of God. Fallen angels were rebels, and against God. They became demons. Satan had been the most treasured angel God had created, but he had turned against God and fallen out of God's graces. His mission was to distract us all from God, so we would burn in eternal hell.

This is the reason those who have had a paranormal encounter or who investigate the paranormal are discriminated against—and even mocked. It's because we are taught that anything of a paranormal nature is of the devil. Most Christians I knew believed encounters from the beyond were from only angels, demons, or the Holy Spirit. So far my experiences didn't fit into Christianity's belief of an afterlife. These encounters confused me.

As I lay in bed reading, the Bible mentioned supernatural occurrences and spiritual gifts. I read in First Corinthians 12:1–11 that Paul talked about spiritual gifts such as the gift of teaching, healing, speaking in tongues, and spiritual discernment. There seemed to be diversity in the gifts that God has given each human being. I also read in Mark 16:9 that Mary Magdalene was the first to see Jesus after his resurrection. Luke 24:36–43 talked about the disciples being terrified of Jesus, believing he was a ghost. Angels appeared to shepherds, and the voice of God appeared in burning bushes. There were so many miracles and supernatural occurrences that I wasn't about to limit God by thinking my experiences were phony. I didn't have an answer yet. So each night before bed, I prayed, asking God for wisdom in my spiritual quest for understanding.

Life continued to flow enjoyably for Hannah and me, although we were living in the upstairs apartment, and I still wanted to be on the ground floor. One day the landlady, Kelly, came to me.

"Jodi, I have good news. A downstairs apartment will be available around the end of January. The last tenants just up and left in the middle of the night, and I never heard from them again. For legal reasons, I had to leave it unoccupied for six months." She then added, "It is right next door to my apartment, and you're welcome to take a look at it later this evening. I will leave it unlocked for you."

Without hesitation, I said, "I will take it."

At around dusk, Hannah and I walked over to take a look around the abandoned apartment. I recall that as I walked in the place, it seemed to be quite cold. I thought to myself, *Well, it is December.* The air in the apartment reminded me of the below-zero weather in Montana. I picked Hannah up, perched her on my hip, and then started to walk down the hallway toward the back bedroom. Though it was just Hannah and me, I had the feeling I wasn't alone. The hair on the back of my neck stood on end, my palms were sweaty, and I felt a strange presence. The experience was similar to the time I walked through the old hospital in Montana. And just like the old hospital, the word "haunted" popped into my mind.

Okay, I am just having an irrational thought. It's because I've been reading the Bible and wondering about spiritual gifts, so I really need to just mellow out and get a grip.

I felt as though we were being followed as we walked throughout the apartment, looking into each eerily empty room. When I walked into the back bedroom, Hannah, still on my hip, waved her hand and said, "Hi, what's your name?"

Her abrupt greeting scared me so badly my heart skipped about three beats, and I wanted to bolt out of the apartment.

"Hannah, who are you talking to?"

"That lady," She said quietly. "She is standing by the window, Mom."

"What lady?"

"I don't know. She was just here, Mom."

"Is she outside the window?" I asked. The back bedroom window didn't have a shade or curtain, so I rationalized she might have seen someone walking by outside.

Hannah then replied, "No, Mom, she was inside. When I blinked my eyes, she was gone."

Chills ran down my back, and I thought for a moment; *there might be someone in the apartment.* But I knew better.

For a split second, my childhood encounter with the Native American boy crossed my mind, but I heard myself say to Hannah, "It was probably a lady walking outside." I didn't want to consider anything other than a rational explanation for what had just occurred.

As we left the apartment, I felt strangely relieved—and warmer. However, I couldn't get what I had just experienced with Hannah out of my mind.

That night, after visiting the apartment, I had a strange and vibrant nightmare—as seemingly real as the one I had experienced when my ghostly grandmother came to visit me, only this time, the setting was from the 1970s, and I felt a sense of foreboding instead of joy.

In the dream, I saw a man in his late teens or early twenties. He was about six feet tall with a thin build and light-brown, shoulder-length hair. His eyes looked dark, and he wore glasses. He was wearing blue jeans with flared bottoms and a thick brown leather belt. From the back, I could see a word on the belt that started with the letter H. Someone was with the man, someone smaller. I couldn't make out any details, but I sensed the person was a woman. Her relation to the man wasn't clear.

A sense of danger loomed in the air as they walked behind an apartment complex. I thought, *Who are these people?* From their conversation, I assumed they were searching for someone. When I looked around, I noticed that the apartment complex looked like mine.

I heard the man say, "She is beautiful—I want this one. Jan, grab the straps and get the head box ready."

The woman said, "How can we get her back to the car without anyone seeing?"

"We will have to wait until dark," the man answered.

I found myself screaming, "No! No!" though I knew I was dreaming. I was terrified something real was happening, and I willed myself awake.

I was disoriented and confused when I opened my eyes. I tried to gather my senses. I remember looking over at my clock: 3:37 in the morning. My body shook uncontrollably with fright as I got up from my bed. I walked over to the window; I needed to make sure it had only been a dream and that the couple wasn't lurking in the bushes outside. I peered out the window and saw no one.

The predatory nature of the couple in the dream had been so incredibly real that I ran over to Hannah. She was sleeping peacefully—until I startled her awake.

"Mama, are you okay?" she cried. "What's wrong?"

I started to cry and said, "I don't know." I couldn't get the monstrous man's image or words he had spoken to the woman—*"Grab the straps and get the head box ready"*—out of my mind. I said breathlessly, "I am worried, honey." Then I grabbed Hannah and ran out my front door and across the hallway. I knocked on my neighbor's door loudly, hoping someone lived there, but no one answered.

I held Hannah tightly, trying to catch my breath. I looked to the right, down the back side of the complex. I felt so scared and sure the couple was still somewhere close by. Still no one answered the door.

My mind was racing with panic and fear, but I was able to calm myself down within a few minutes. I told myself it was only a dream. My heart slowly gained a regular beat again, and my mind calmed down.

Hannah, hugging me tight, was staring at me with confused little eyes, crying, "Mama, Mama!" I realized, as I looked at her tearful expression, that I was acting irrationally. What was I expecting the neighbors to do? For Hannah's sake, I regained my composure and calmly walked back to my apartment.

As I walked through my front door, I let out a deep sigh and sat down on the living room floor with Hannah next to me. I cried to God, "Help me! Please erase that crazy nightmare from my memory—take it away!" I was alone and terrified of a couple who may or may not have existed...but they had seemed so real.

"Mama, are you okay?" Hannah asked. "Why are you scared?"

Having gathered myself, I replied, "I am fine, honey, I just had a bad dream, about some scary people."

Hannah reached over and hugged me, looked into my eyes and said, "Mommy, God will protect us from scary people." I felt foolish and childlike for being so scared about a dream. Hannah fell asleep in my arms as we lay on the living room floor.

When daylight finally broke, I felt a tremendous amount of relief. The sunshine somehow calmed my nerves, and I was able to finally fall asleep alongside Hannah. Later that morning, I awoke feeling relieved, yet mystified by my reaction and the vividness of the dream. I decided to call Jenny to get her take.

My grounded, practical friend had a sensible answer. "Jodi, come on girl, it was only a nightmare. You know you're moving again, and that's probably causing you to subconsciously stress."

"I don't think it's stress," I replied. "Something about the dream was too real. I can't really explain it, other than it was similar to the encounter I had with my grandmother when she announced Hannah's birth. It was that real, Jenny."

Again she said, "It was only a nightmare."

Talking to Jenny put my emotions and fears to rest, but I couldn't get the face, or words, of the strange man out of my mind.

SIX

The Clues

On January 29, 2000, I had just finished signing the lease to the downstairs apartment when Kelly said, "Why don't you and Hannah take a few of your things to the apartment? The new carpet is finally finished."

It was almost dark, and I was anxious to get things rolling, so I said, "Yeah, that's a good idea. I have most of my stuff in boxes. I'll head over after dinner."

When Hannah and I walked through the front door of our new home, the smell of new paint and carpet overwhelmed me, but the apartment looked so much better than before that I didn't care. Through the hallway and to the bedroom we went, with me carrying a box of our possessions. Once in the bedroom, I decided to open the window to get some fresh air. I put the box in the walk-in closet and then sat on the floor with Hannah. Everything seemed just fine, only empty.

We lay on the floor, talking and laughing awhile, but I couldn't help thinking about the last time I had been there with Hannah—when she had said "hi" to a mysterious girl, or the strange couple I had encountered in my dream that same night.

After a while, I decided it was time to head back upstairs to do more packing. My daughter and I held hands as we walked through the hallway to the front room.

I remember her saying, "Mama, laying on the floor with you was fun. I like our new place, but I didn't say goodbye to the lady." I cringed and thought, *Oh my God, did she see the girl again? Please, God, not again.*

We were now back upstairs, tired and ready for bed.

That evening, my nightmare returned. The same man from the seventies, with his light-brown hair and glasses, made another appearance, and so did his accomplice. During this dream, I witnessed the couple talking with a young girl who looked about eighteen to twenty years old; she was beautiful and had a slim figure and brown hair just past her shoulders. I couldn't make out her face, but by her silhouette, she looked as though she could have been a model.

The couple was parked on the side of what looked to be a familiar tree-lined street in Chico, though at that moment, my mind could not name it. The couple sat in a small blue car as the girl leaned over and talked to them. Before long, I saw her get into the car, and they all drove off.

During my dream, the three engaged in chitchat. I heard the woman in the front seat say, "You're beautiful. Are you a model?" The young, beautiful thin woman in the backseat said, "Yeah, actually I am. I did some modeling for a couple of stores recently." The woman in the front seat said, "Oooh, that sounds fun." I could see that the man in the front seat was staring at the woman in the rearview mirror. Then I heard the girl in the back seat say, "My place is just down the road from here."

After arriving at their destination, all three people got out of the small, blue car. The odd-looking smaller woman, who wore horn-rimmed glasses, said, "We have been driving a while, would it be okay if we used your bathroom?"

"Sure, my apartment is just over here."

The three were now inside the young woman's apartment. I heard the woman say, "Can I offer you something to drink?"

Both the man and woman replied, "Yes, thank you."

The small woman with glasses sat at the kitchen table while the man excused himself to use the bathroom.

I heard the younger woman say, "It's down the hall and to your left."

I saw him get up and stand behind the young woman with something in his hand. The strange woman with glasses looked up at the man and then gave him a signal. He pulled a cloth and what looked to be a bottle of eye drops from his pocket. He squirted what was in the bottle on the rag, reached around, and put a cloth over the young girl's mouth. She struggled for breath and then fell from her chair to her knees.

I was scared and panicked—I wanted to wake up, but I couldn't. The young woman was conscious, but barely able to move. They both picked her up by the arms and guided her steps toward the front door. She looked drunk.

The woman with the glasses opened the front door and looked out. Then she turned to the man and said, "I don't see anyone. Why don't you pull the car next to the curb? I'll wait here—hurry!"

The man walked back to the blue car, got in, and parked next to a curb right next to the back side of what I then realized was my apartment complex. I wanted to stop them, but I couldn't—I didn't know what to do. I saw the man reach in the back seat and lift up some kind of square box with foam in it.

He rushed back to the front door and said, "Jan, hurry—we need to fit this on her head before she wakes."

I willed myself awake, and I awoke to myself screaming, "No!"

I startled Hannah awake, and she started to cry. "Mama…Mama!"

I grabbed the phone and dialed Jenny. My heart was racing, and Hannah was crying. I heard the phone ringing, but my friend didn't answer. I was having a panic attack. I glanced over at the clock, and it read 3:37 in the morning—the exact same time as my last nightmare.

Finally, Jenny answered. I was crying and out of breath. "Jenny, Jenny, help me!"

"Jodi, what's wrong?" she sounded afraid, as I had clearly startled her. "Is there an emergency? Is Hannah okay?"

I broke down crying and blurted out, "It's the nightmare again!"

"Whew! Is that all, Jodi?" Jenny exclaimed in an irritated voice. It was 3:37 a.m., after all.

"Yes…I had the nightmare again. What is wrong with me? Do you think someone is after Hannah or me?"

"Why would you think such a thing?"

"I don't know. I keep dreaming about a strange couple, stalking and stealing young women! Maybe God is trying to tell me something though my dreams—maybe Hannah's going to being abducted!"

"Come on Jodi, do you really think that someone is out to steal your child? You're just freaking out because you're moving again."

As painful as the nightmare had been, I needed to get a grip. For God's sake, I used to live in Montana, with real danger like below-freezing weather, bears, and lions, not to mention my alcoholic mother. This was simply a strange nightmare.

"Jenny, I really don't know what is going on with me. I've never had such real and vivid dreams." She stayed on the phone with me until I calmed down. When we hung up, I wondered if I was simply stressed out or going insane.

The next day, I woke up confused, but remained focused on packing and moving. I had arranged for a few friends and a couple of young men from the complex to help me. I had everything taken to my new place except my bed—I had decided Hannah and I would spend one last night upstairs. I had only been in Chico for a few weeks, and here I was after two months upstairs, moving again.

That last night upstairs, I lay in bed thinking over the past year. I had moved from Montana to Chico with high expectations. I anticipated life to be comfortable and full of peace. Since Montana, I had struggled with worries, little money, single motherhood. I closed my eyes and said a prayer: "God, please give me peace and understanding."

I never entertained the idea on a conscious level that my daughter and I were going to become characters in a life-altering, full-blown mystery—a mystery that spanned the past thirty-plus years. And a mystery that would lead me to question what life after death really means. Living upstairs at my apartment complex was only the beginning, I would soon find out.

SEVEN

First Night Downstairs

I moved downstairs on February 1, 2000. The apartment was cute and cozy, with exactly the same floor plan as the upstairs unit. A friend of Jenny's was moving out of town and knew I needed household items, so she donated them to me. Jenny and I took the things and decorated the apartment. There were beautiful, handmade quilted pillows, houseplants, and candles to adorn the hand-me-down coffee table Jenny had given me. Jenny also gave us two small, old-school TVs—the kind with an actual dial to change channels. I put one in the living room and one in my bedroom.

Everything looked comfortable and inviting, but still, I felt strangely uncomfortable. A sense of impending doom lingered in the air, and I couldn't figure out why.

I was very particular about a few things upon moving in: keys went on hooks next to the phone, and shoes and a diaper bag were always placed next to the door, ready to go. Organization made my life as a single mother run a bit more smoothly. One strange quirk I had acquired over the years was my need to have four clocks throughout my apartment: one in the kitchen, one in the living room, and two in my bedroom. My grandmother, a bookkeeper by trade, had taught me to be time-conscious. When you live in the mountains, a battery-operated clock is a must, because the electricity might go out. Though I was now living in the city, the clock fixation continued to follow me—hence the four clocks, with the one in the living room and the one in my bedroom running on batteries, and the others were plugged in.

Because I was feeling so strange, I decided to walk throughout the apartment with Hannah to make sure each room was in order. Maybe I could shake the uneasy feelings by acquainting myself with my new surroundings. We went through the hallway and over to Hannah's playroom, which was cute and pink, filled with toys. She had one special toy in particular that had traveled with us from Montana to Chico, a "Sing and Snore Ernie" doll. It was a gift given to Hannah on her first Christmas. When someone picked it up, it would say, "I love you," "I feel great," and "Hug me, please." When laid back down, it would snore; after a minute, the computer chip inside would deactivate until the doll was picked up again. Hannah loved that doll and carried it around with her daily.

As Hannah and I walked into her pink room, she said, "Mama, make sure Ernie has a special place to sit."

"How about we set him on top of your dresser?" I responded.

"That sounds like a good spot for him. Then I won't lose him." Ernie now had a coveted seat on top of a lovely white antique dresser in Hannah's room. The other toys, however, weren't as lucky; they shared a trunk beneath the window. Her room was sparse, but that allowed her to have space to play. Since we shared a bed, the availability of a playroom seemed important.

After walking throughout the apartment, I felt a little better and decided to light a candle. I asked Hannah if she wanted to watch some TV with me. We lay on the couch, watching the TV and resting.

Unfortunately, the feeling of well-being didn't last long. Soon the atmosphere in the apartment became tense and heavy—and I couldn't figure out why. It made the hair on the back of my neck stand up. I told myself, *It's only your imagination. Stop freaking out.*

All of a sudden I started choking and couldn't catch my breath—it felt as though I had a pair of hands wrapped around my neck. Luckily, I was able to gather my senses and told myself I was having a panic attack because it was a new environment. I reasoned it must be the fumes from the carpet or the new paint that had caused me to choke and feel breathless.

Even if that were the case, I still couldn't figure why it felt like someone was actually choking me. From my very first visit to the downstairs apartment, something hadn't seemed right. I was supposed to feel safer in the downstairs apartment, but I was feeling anxious and uneasy.

I decided to call Jenny. Maybe she could help calm my nerves.

"Hi, Jenny. I was having trouble relaxing, so I thought I would call. For some unknown reason, I feel anxious." I didn't mention anything about being choked.

I sensed some hesitation in Jenny's voice, then she kind of nonchalantly said, "Jodi, I didn't want to alarm you, since you been stressed out lately, but while in your apartment decorating alone for a few minutes, I had a strange feeling someone was watching me, though nobody was in the apartment. I looked throughout the apartment, but just as I suspected, I was alone."

Okay, great! I thought to myself. Not only am I feeling strange in this apartment, but my good friend Jenny also had a strange and uncomfortable experience. At that point, I was trying to remain calm and to determine whether Jenny and I were both complete nut jobs. I was hoping there was a reasonable explanation for the anomalies.

"You know Jenny, I had a similar experience. Do you think it's the chemicals from the paint or the carpet?"

"I have no idea, but I do know that some people pay a lot of money to have a high like that," Jenny said,

We laughed, and then I said, "Well, if that's the case, maybe we should charge people for touring my apartment."

"Or we're both insane," she countered, "and should check ourselves into the nearest insane asylum." We both had a good chuckle and chalked our strange experiences up to paint fumes and the stress of moving.

Talking with Jenny put my mind and nerves at ease, at least for the time being. I was now able to settle into a milder state of mind and laugh at myself.

Our conversation ended at around 11 p.m. Since Hannah had fallen asleep on the couch, I decided it best if we slept there. The laugh with Jenny seemed to be the perfect dose of medicine I needed. All seemed well and I too drifted off into a deep sleep next to Hannah.

That night, I had yet another vivid, mysterious dream. I was in a meadow scattered with lava rocks. As I looked around, I could tell the location was rural. I noticed one particular lava rock that was four feet tall and three feet wide. Behind the rock was freshly turned-over dirt with a small piece of what looked like the edge of a blanket sticking out. While in the meadow, I noticed some trees and a creek behind me; off to the right, I could see snow-capped mountains. When I looked at the ground where I stood, I noticed a small, gray Pacific Gas and Electric marker next to me. It read "A17."

After assessing the land, I heard the words "35.76 miles northeast of Red Bluff, California." I looked around to see who had spoken them; it sounded like a young woman's voice. However, I didn't see anyone. I then heard a whisper in my ear: "Wake up!" And I did.

I woke up to the "Sing and Snore Ernie" doll on the floor next to us, screaming, "I feel great! I feel great! I feel great!" I just about jumped out of my skin. I was scared and confused. Every light in the apartment—bedroom, kitchen, living room—had been turned on. And the volume on the TV was turned up full blast. Three pillows had also been stacked neatly next to my head. When I looked up at the clock, it read 3:37.

My heart was racing, my lips were numb, I felt as if I was choking again, and I couldn't catch my breath.

Hannah started screaming, "Mama, Mama, what's going on?" I wanted to run out the front door, but I was too scared to move. I looked around at all the chaos and started to cry with panic. I didn't know what was going on. For a minute, I thought I might be having a nightmare, but I was awake. I told myself to calm down.

I looked around and thought, *there must be a logical reason for this situation*. Hannah was staring at me with tear-filled eyes. I knew I needed to comfort her.

"Don't worry, honey," I said. "There must be an electrical problem. Let's see what's going on."

I gathered my senses and headed down the hallway to the electrical breaker. I thought there must have been a power surge. As I walked down the hallway, I noticed it was extremely cold—cold enough to see my breath. The eeriness made the hair on the back of neck stand on end.

Though I was terrified, I continued my walk. I opened up the electrical breaker, and everything looked fine.

"Mama, why is the bedroom TV on?" Hannah asked.

I looked over to my right, into my bedroom. She was right: My TV was on—no picture, just white static blasting at full volume. I trembled. The overhead light and the light on top of my dresser were on as well. Both the living room and bedroom TVs had knob dials for volume, so I couldn't understand how they could be on. Nothing made sense.

"Maybe it was that girl who was here before," she said. "Maybe she turned on the lights, Mommy."

I was frustrated and scared. "Hannah, now's not the time for imaginary friends!"

"Mommy, I'm sorry!" she cried out.

Hannah had never mentioned imaginary friends, ever! It was very unlike her to pretend—not to mention extremely unnerving in the moment. I felt bad that I had let my terror affect my reaction to her innocent response. I hugged her.

"Sorry, honey. Mommy didn't mean to yell at you; it's that I just don't understand how everything could be on right now sweetie."

At this point, I really wanted to run out my front door screaming. However, I thought that if I did, the neighbors might call the police. Somehow, in that strange moment,

I was reminded of my earlier conversation with Jenny. I started to laugh and cry at the same time, in hysterics. Through the experience was strange, I thought, *Now's not a good time to be locked in a loony bin, drooling—especially without my good friend Jenny. After all that happened, most likely it was a power surge of some kind, right?*

I could rationalize the problem away as electrical, but I couldn't find any explanation for the Ernie doll screaming or the three pillows stacked next to my head. Then there was the strange dream and voice waking me up at exactly 3:37 a.m. *What could all of this mean?* This was the first time in my life anything had manifested in a physical manner. I didn't know what to think or do.

Confused and tired after the strange and worrisome incident, I decided to pray. While I walked back to the couch, I asked God for the protection of my home. I lay down with Hannah and thought that I would get to the bottom of this craziness in the morning. I tried to fall asleep, but it was impossible. I lay there confused and in terror, not sure if I was insane or if something was really wrong in the apartment.

Morning arrived, and I hadn't slept a wink. During the night, I had convinced myself the frightening experience had been a power surge—nothing more, but something I should address with the manager after breakfast.

Late in the morning, I decided to go talk with Kelly, the apartment manager. When Hannah and I walked through the front door, Kelly was quietly doing paperwork.

She smiled and asked how my first night in the new place had been.

I said with a little laugh, "Well, Kelly, I had a fun night filled with all the excitement of a roller-coaster ride and a virgin on prom night!"

I began telling her what had occurred with the lights and TVs and mentioned how it was unnerving to wake up to such a weird occurrence at 3:37 in the morning.

"That power outage we had last night sure threw me for a loop," I added.

Kelly laughed. "Jodi, I'm not aware of any power outage or surge last night in the complex." She continued, "If those things had happened to me, I might have wanted to run out my front door screaming as well."

I laughed and thought to myself, *Thank God I'm not the only one—whew!*

After a bit of humorous conversation, she agreed to have my apartment's electricity checked out to put my mind at ease—that way I would be assured of a peaceful night's rest and wouldn't feel like running out the front door screaming if something like that occurred again.

Feeling relieved, I went back to the apartment and waited for the electrician. Three hours passed before he arrived. With tools and equipment in hand, he walked through the whole apartment, looking at lamps, lights, TVs, and anything else inside that needed to be checked out. He then made his way outside to check on all the outside boxes and breakers. After assessing all possible electrical issues, he came back inside with a diagnosis.

"Everything looks normal," he said. "Sometimes these things happen and there isn't an explanation for it. You and your family are electrically okay."

I wondered if he talked this way to everyone. I ignored his patronizing tone and asked, "Sir, are you sure that everything is okay, that there is not one thing wrong in the apartment? I know this sounds strange, but is there any possible way a TV with a knob dial for volume could all of a sudden turn up full blast when it was completely off when we went to bed?"

"Miss," he replied, "as far as I know, that is impossible." He looked at me as though I had horns growing from my head then added, "Maybe it was your daughter." His condescending comments bothered me a bit, but I was glad to hear everything on the home front was okay.

I felt relieved and unnerved at the same time. I couldn't for the life of me understand what might cause such strange occurrences at 3:37 a.m., and from what Kelly said, the strange issue had been limited to only my apartment.

As the electrician left, I started to laugh at myself, and thought *maybe I should sign up for some medication and a mental-health evaluation.* However, I was holding out hope that there was an explanation—other than insanity—regarding the previous night's bizarre occurrence.

After a good belly laugh, I thought it best to just get back to normal housework and other everyday life. Everything seemed calm now as dusk descended and rain fell. I noticed a beautiful water pattern cascading down the sliding-glass window in my living room while I stood in the kitchen, preparing dinner. Somehow it reminded me of God's constant presence. I decided to pray while I cooked.

My Christian upbringing, the experience with my grandma, the nightmares, and now the strange occurrence in my apartment dominated my thoughts. Most Christians I knew didn't believe in these kinds of experiences, or if they did, it was explained as the devil beckoning you to stray you away from God. I recalled once again the conversation with Ryan about his Native American belief in an afterlife and the conversations with my grandfather as a child. I wondered if I were crazy, if they were crazy, or if the Christians were right and the devil really was out to get me.

I really needed an explanation for my experiences; I started to pray: "Dear God, I am really freaking out and I need to know if I am crazy or not. Why on earth would I have such strange anomalies, dreams, feelings?"

During that prayer, the afterlife really dominated my thoughts, and I honestly didn't know why. I said, "God, can spirits really come back to talk to us like my grandpa explained to me as a child? I have had so many strange things happen to me over my life regarding the supernatural, am I crazy?"

When I had first arrived in Chico, I remember calling the neighborhood church to ask if they knew of any reasonably priced apartments for rent. A nice woman answered the phone and chatted with me a while. She gave me the names of a few places to check out, and also invited me to visit their church. I recall explaining how I had recently moved from Montana to Chico, and how I suffered with panic attacks. I told her that being around large crowds of people sometimes freaked me out. She understood and suggested under the circumstances that someone might be able to come to my home and visit and pray with me. While I stood in the kitchen cooking and praying, I considered reaching out again, for support, but I was reluctant due to fear of judgment.

I believed God worked in mysterious ways, and from the magical day when I asked Jesus into my heart (at the ripe old age of nine) until present, I continued to identify as a Christian. Due to my experience as a child, and now as an adult, I was beginning to think that what might look as though it is negative, bad, or from the devil might simply be a matter of perception!

Over the years, and because of my unusual experiences, I was starting to doubt what I was being taught in organized churches, but I really didn't know who or where to turn to, other than spiritual books on religions, and also the Bible. After reading night after night, in the upstairs apartment, I was starting to believe in the core truths of all religions. I believed that God was within everyone's heart and soul! And also started to really believe that the knowingness in the pit of everyone heart/stomach was where God did indeed reside. Unfortunately, some of my Christian friends didn't agree with me, so I felt extremely isolated.

I recalled a passage in Bible in which Jesus was walking on water and the disciples thought he was a ghost (Matt. 14:26). The disciples' worldview thousands of years ago allowed for spirits. As I stood there in my kitchen, I started to think about the Bible, and how it talked about prophets, oracles, dreams, visits from angels and demons, astrology, and more. What I didn't understand was that if the Bible talked about such things, why didn't the church or Christians recognize them?

As I read and prayed, I kept thinking that there seemed to be central themes in all religions and cultures: the belief in God, an afterlife, and supernatural phenomenon. And these experiences usually came in a time of need or great distress, and changed or challenged the way those affected viewed faith, life, and existence.

I didn't realize it at the time, but after moving to the downstairs apartment, and for the next thirty days and nights, life, as I viewed it thus far, would be changed forever, and I was soon going to come to terms with my abilities and gifts. I was going to soon understand that God gives each and every one of us special experiences and gifts.

It was now 6:00 p.m. I was exhausted from the day's events and previous night's adventures. I walked over to the sliding-glass window to take a peek outside. It was extremely dark and gloomy. The sky was filled with rain clouds that made for an eerie environment. I started to feel claustrophobic and tense, so even though it was raining, I opened the sliding-glass door to let some fresh air in.

As I stood at the window, I heard the phone ring and walked over to the kitchen and answered it. It was my friend Kathy. Kathy and her kids had been my neighbors in Chico before my grandma died. Kathy and I had connected on the phone a few times since I had been back, but I had not yet seen her or her sixteen-year-old daughter Jessica.

"Hello, Jodi," she said. "Jessica and I were wondering if we could stop by and say hi, and if it's okay with you she would love to stay the night and catch up on everything that has happened since you moved away."

Before I moved away to Montana, Jessica would come over to my house and help me do chores, and spend time with me and grandma.

Kathy said she could only stay a minute because she had a Bible study to attend, but she would love it if Jessica could stay the night with me. She added: "I have been really busy, and I could really use some alone time."

After the previous night's excitement, I welcomed the idea of company.

"Of course she can stay," I said. "I would actually love the company. Go ahead and take some much-needed mom time. Jessica can catch you up on my moving adventures later."

When I hung up the phone, I took a much-needed deep sigh of relief, and the tension I had been feeling, lessened knowing I wouldn't be alone tonight.

Thunder and rain continued for the next hour and half. It was about seven-thirty when I heard a knock on the door. When I opened the front door, standing in the doorway were Kathy and Jessica. I smiled and said, "Oh my goodness Jessica, you have grown. Please come on in."

Kathy stood in my doorway, keys in hand, and said, "It's so good to see you and Hannah, but I can't come in, honey. I am running late."

I noticed she was wearing a blue hooded sweatshirt with a pocket in the front.

"No problem," I said. "It will be nice to have company tonight. Things have been a little strange lately."

"How so?" Kathy replied.

"Last night, at 3:37 in the morning, I woke up to the lights and TVs being turned on. An electrician came to check the breakers and told me everything was okay."

Still standing in the doorway of the apartment, Kathy jokingly said, "Maybe this apartment is haunted."

Jessica laughed and walked inside and agreed. "Yeah, Mom, that's it—the place is haunted." Jessica sat on the living room floor to play with Hannah and the coveted Ernie doll. Kathy, still standing in the doorway, turned to leave when she said in surprise, "Where are my keys? They were just in my hand."

I had seen the keys in her hand while she was standing in the doorway. She had never moved away from or out of the doorway—not even once. In fact, we had both stood there talking and laughing together, never moving an inch. She put her hands in her pocket to feel for the keys, but she couldn't find them. I even stuck my hands in her pockets to help her look for the keys and also came up empty-handed. Kathy and I both checked all the pockets of her clothing. There weren't any keys to be found. We looked on the ground, and found nothing.

"Jessica, did you take my keys, or see where the keys went?" Kathy asked.

"No, Mom. Hannah and I have been sitting here the whole time."

Right then, the sound of thunder made an abrupt boom like a cannon going go off, and rain started to come down in buckets. The thunder had sent a bolt of adrenaline into the center of my being and I started to shake.

Though I was shaking, Kathy and I kept looking around the floor, never moving from the doorway, when all of a sudden, she reached back into her sweatshirt and found them in the right pocket.

I shook my head nervously and asked, "How is that even possible? You just had your keys in your hand—how could they mysteriously end up in your pocket? We both looked there at least twice."

Kathy started laughing. "I don't know," she said. "Are we both losing our minds, or is your house haunted?"

I laughed, yet cringed inside, and said, "Why would you think my house is haunted?"

Kathy giggled with nervousness and then said, "Oh I don't know, it's just a word. I hope nothing else strange happens to you gals tonight." The word "haunted" hit me like a bolt of lightning, and I thought it strange that Kathy, a devout Christian, used the word to describe something strange and unusual. She left shaking her head and said, "Jessica, call if you or Jodi need anything."

After Kathy left, the girls and I settled in for the night, watching TV and listening to the rain fall outside. Jessica said she was getting tired, so I told her she could sleep in my room, and that Hannah and I would sleep in the living room. She agreed and headed off to bed. After a few minutes, I walked back to the bedroom and tucked her in, turned off all the lights, and kissed her good night. It was about 11:30 p.m.

I walked throughout the whole apartment, conscious about turning off all the lights and making sure all TVs and lamps were off. My mind raced as I thought about the incident with Kathy's keys and her comment about my house being haunted. As I lay down on the couch with Hannah, the only thing I had left on in the apartment was the bathroom light.

Since the electrician had assured me that there were no problems with lights, electrical boxes, or breakers, I felt confident that we were electrically okay and that I didn't have to worry about another incident like the previous night. I was also thankful that I had Jessica's company to ease the loneliness.

Before I fell asleep, I prayed that we would all have a peaceful and comforting night's sleep, and added, "Grams, if you are out there, please watch over us and be my guardian angel tonight."

I listened to the rain fall and distant thunder as I lay there with Hannah drifting off to sleep.

The next thing I remember was Jessica shaking me awake from a sound sleep.

"Jodi, Jodi, wake up! I am freaking out!"

"What's wrong, honey? Are you okay?" I yelled.

"No. No! I had been lying in the dark, trying to sleep," Jessica said, "when suddenly the overhead lights turned on by themselves. It scared me, so I sat up, and when I did, the mini-blinds on the window flew up. I ran out of the room!"

"What?" I said, trying to gather my wits. "What are you talking about?"

As I got up, I looked at the clock. Once again, it read 3:37 a.m. I took a deep breath and said in my mind: *Don't panic. There is a logical explanation for this.*

EIGHT

Childhood Memories

It was unpleasantly cold, dark, and mystifying. The moon was sheltered by the murky, looming clouds. The rain and thunder had stopped, yet I felt anxious and uneasy. It was just a little past 4:00 a.m. Jessica, Hannah, and I decided to sleep together; we were trying to regroup after the strange occurence. But it was next to impossible to remain calm and peaceful after all the excitement. I remember shaking like a frightened little girl, holding both Hannah and Jessica on each side of me. I peered out from underneath the covers that I had pulled up to my nose. My wall heater for a brief time seemed to be offering respite from the storm inside and outside. I looked out my window and just gazed, my mind wandering in all directions. I dwelled on the treacherous possibilities regarding what had just happened.

I said to myself, *Something is wrong—very wrong. God please keep us safe.* In the pit of my stomach, I felt an overwhelming sense of loss—the same kind of loss, grief, and confusion I had felt after my grandpa had died. As I lay there, I realized that a feeling of loss emanated throughout the entire apartment, and it had since I had moved in. I couldn't comprehend the reality of the situation, or what could be going on since I had moved in, but I prayed for peace and understanding. Right then, I had a great revelation, and for the first time ever, I thought, *Something paranormal is going on in the apartment.*

"Jessica, are you okay?" I asked.

"That was really strange," she responded. "How could something so weird happen?"

"I don't know, honey," I said. "This is the second night in a row something strange has happened."

"Maybe we are both crazy." Jessica laughed and said, "I know this will sound strange, Jodi, but I felt like someone was watching me."

"You're not the only one who felt like that. Jenny had a similar experience." I laughed. "Maybe we could all go to the funny farm on a family plan."

Though we hadn't slept, Jessica needed to get to school, and I wanted to get out of the apartment. I figured I could drop her off at school and then head over to Jenny's. The dark, gray, overcast morning caused a gloomy mood. As I stepped out of the house, I began to shiver. An extremely cold wind was blowing. The girls and I bundled up and walked quietly to my car. My nose began to run, and my ears were as cold as ice.

"Mommy it's so cold, I feel it in my bones," Hannah said. Suddenly clouds began to thunder and lightning began to flash.

"Hurry girls," I said, "before we get drenched." We got into the car and drove to our destinations.

When I arrived at Jenny's house, it was calm, peaceful, and inviting. Inside, she gave me a cup of hot, steaming tea and covered me with a quilt—I was shivering with cold and anxiety from the previous night's adventure. I sat next to her warm heater with Hannah on my lap, warming my hands. I felt lucky to have her as my good friend and confidant.

"Are you and Hannah hungry?"

"I am not sure," I answered, "but if you're cooking, I'm eating." Our kids played while Jenny whipped up some bacon and eggs. As we stood in her kitchen, I looked around. Her house was warm and cozy. I wondered if she had ever experienced any strange anomalies.

I was so caught up in my own thought that I blurted out, "Jenny, do you believe in the spiritual realm?"

Startled, Jenny replied, "That is a strange thing to ask out of the blue. Why?"

"Yeah I know, it's just that I have been thinking about spiritual issues and religion." I didn't want to tell her that suddenly I believed that paranormal anomalies were occurring in my apartment.

"Well Jodi, I believe wholeheartedly that there are different realms of existence," Jenny said. "I actually have a cousin who is a psychic. My family was raised Catholic, but my grandfather was a medicine man and healer over in Cuba who practiced Santería."

This was the first time Jenny and I had ever talked about our religious backgrounds.

"Wow, Jenny—that's interesting. So you have a psychic and a medicine man in your family! How do Catholicism and Santería, two seemingly different religious ideas, blend together?"

"Both evolved out of our family traditions," she answered.

Although interesting, this new information didn't really explain to me why my lights all of a sudden turned on during the night or how clocks and mini-blinds could be tampered with.

Jenny continued. "For some reason I felt like I should pray for you and Hannah, and your new apartment, last night. There's something strange going on in there."

My stomach sank, and my heart raced. I knew it. I think we all knew it deep inside, but we didn't know what it was or how to deal with it yet. This was before all the TV shows about ghost hunting and the paranormal, so talking about the supernatural or a haunted location was still a bit out of the ordinary.

After a while, I said, "There is something so heavy about the burden that lies ahead. I am strong, but I am tired. Jenny,

I don't know if I have the strength to figure this out on my own."

I shifted uncomfortably in my seat, and continued. "I'm tired of pretending, tired of acting like everything's okay. It's not! Since moving into the apartment, I have had nightmares, electrical problems, mini-blinds flying up, and strange paranormal events. Maybe I am crazy."

"Jodi, you're not crazy. I have known you for a long time, but maybe to ease your mind, you should get some counseling." She suggested I go to the local county's mental-health program clinic; which was right around the corner from my apartment complex.

"You know, I think that is a great idea," I said. "It couldn't hurt, and you're right. It might ease my mind."

I thanked Jenny for the conversation, food, warmth, and much-needed company. Then Hannah and I left.

On our way home, Hannah reminded me she had to stop by the store for a gift because she had been invited to a birthday party on Saturday. Since Hannah loved her "Sing and Snore Ernie" doll so much, she wanted to give one to her friend. We stopped off at the local toy store and picked up the exact same doll for her friend.

Driving home from the store that evening, I remember feeling anxious and afraid. After the past few days and nights, I was worried about what I might encounter at the apartment. I was hoping everything would be exactly the way I had left it—I didn't want any surprises. I drove into the parking lot and stopped. I took in a deep breath, got out of my car, and took Hannah out of her car seat. Apprehensive and frightened, I walked to the apartment with Hannah on my hip, worried about what I might encounter.

To my surprise, when I walked into my house, I found everything exactly the way I had left it. What a relief!

I was now at home, feeling warm and safe. Hannah and I settled in to enjoy dinner and some playtime. I was tired and looking forward to a good night's sleep.

But before heading off to bed that night, I intentionally took a good look around the apartment, assessing all the clocks and lights. Things had been so strange the past few days, I wanted to make sure all the lights and TVs worked, and were turned off. I made sure all windows and doors were in working order, locked, and secured. I needed peace of mind and to know that my home was safe.

On our way to bed, Hannah and I put the new Ernie doll on the top shelf in the back bedroom closet. I felt broken down and consumed with the strange occurrences I had been experiencing thus far, and I practically collapsed as Hannah and I lay our heads down to sleep.

In the middle of the night, I awoke to a loud noise coming from the closet. At first I thought I was dreaming, but as I gathered my senses, I realized it was the Ernie doll. It was screaming, "I feel great! I feel great! I feel great!"

I knew something was wrong, but in that moment, I somehow convinced myself it must be the batteries in the doll that were bad. In the darkness, I made my way into the closet.

I switched on the closet light and grabbed the doll, which was continuing to yell, "I feel great...I feel great...I feel great!" When I picked it up, it immediately stopped yelling. I was freaked out and shaken. It was a new doll, but it did the same thing as Hannah's other Ernie doll had done. What was going on? Was I going nuts? Had I lost my mind? Should I run around the corner to the mental-health clinic?

Hannah had been startled awake from the noise as well. She sat up in bed and asked, "Why is the new Ernie screaming so loud?"

I started to cry. I didn't have an answer for her. All I could say was, "Honey, it must be the batteries."

She looked over at me and calmly said, "Mommy, we will be okay. My angel is in the corner, watching over us."

I looked over to the clock. It was 3:37 a.m.

"Why? *Why?*" I yelled into the air. I tried to make sense of this anomaly. I looked around, shaking with fright. I felt my arms tremble as I reached up to put the doll back on the shelf.

Hannah looked over at me. Crying, I sat on the closet floor in despair.

"Mommy, my angel didn't want to scare us. She woke Ernie up so we would know she was here. She will be quiet now, so we can sleep." She then said, "It's time for bed. Let's say a prayer and ask God to help us sleep."

I didn't know what to do. I said, "What angel? Who is the angel?" This was the first time Hannah had ever mentioned an angel to me.

"God gave her to me." Hannah replied.

"What are you talking about Hannah? Now's not a good time for stories," I said through tears. I was at my wit's end; I couldn't take the strange occurrences any longer.

I got up off the floor, walked over to the bed, and hugged my child. I whispered into her ear as I lay down with her, "Hannah, I love you so much." And I prayed, "God, it's only day four in the apartment. Every night so far, I have experienced some kind of strange, unexplainable anomaly. I can't take it much longer." So far, I had experienced lights turning off and on, two different Ernie dolls screaming, my friend's keys disappearing and then reappearing, and miniblinds flying up on their own. I couldn't explain any of it. Nothing made sense.

The only thing that kept me from thinking I was completely insane was the fact that Jenny, Hannah, Jessica, and Kathy had also experienced the strange anomalies. I really wanted to talk to a counselor as soon as possible. I needed a professional opinion—I knew something was wrong, and I needed to get to the bottom of this.

I was encountering frightening oddities I had never experienced before. I knew there must be a reasonable explanation. I was pretty sure the answer wasn't going to be that Jenny, Hannah, Jessica, Kathy, and I were all nuts.

A plethora of thoughts flooded my mind: Santería, Catholicism, psychics, Christian beliefs, and Native American religion. Confused, I wondered if there could be an answer in any one religion, or if there could be an answer in a meeting with a professional counselor.

The following morning, I decided to call the local county's mental-health program.

A receptionist answered and said, "I am sorry, but we have a waiting list. It will be a month before I can book you an appointment." I was disappointed. The receptionist added, "If you need immediate help, you could go to the inpatient unit."

Although I was feeling confused about all the excitement in my apartment, I knew I didn't need to be a patient at a mental hospital—not yet, anyway.

"Thank you, but for now, I just want to schedule an appointment," I said. Since I couldn't get in to see a counselor for a month, I needed a plan in case things didn't change. I thought about moving again, but I was living off my savings from Montana, and money was tight. I assumed there was a rational explanation for the occurrences, but just in case getting to the bottom of the situation took a while, I called Kathy and asked her if Jessica could stay with me for a couple of weeks, and she agreed. I also called Jenny and shared my plan with her. I didn't want to feel like a passive victim to the strangeness any longer.

My next step was to talk to Kelly without sounding completely loony. I walked over to her apartment next door and knocked. Kelly had been visiting her boyfriend for a couple of days and wasn't aware that the anomalies had continued.

"Come in," Kelly replied. "I was just making some hot cocoa. Would you and Hannah like a cup?"

"That sounds good—I would love one."

"Make yourselves comfortable," Kelly said.

We sat at her kitchen table. I wasn't sure how to address my apartment issues. I was waiting for the perfect moment.

"So how do you and Hannah like the new downstairs apartment?" Kelly asked.

I saw a good opportunity to broach the topic.

"Well, Kelly," I said, "I am getting used to lights being turned on in different rooms during the night between 2:00 a.m. and 5:00 a.m., although I am still having trouble getting used to Hannah's Ernie doll screaming loudly in the middle of the night."

She looked at me as though my head had just made a 360-degree rotation. "Jodi, what in the world are you talking about?"

I cleared my throat. "I don't really know what is going on. I can't really explain it." Then I started to cry. "I know we had the electricity looked at in the apartment, and everything was okay...but strange things keep happening in my apartment." Kelly looked at me as though I had now grown horns out of my head. "I know this sounds crazy, but somehow, these strange occurrences happen during the early-morning hours—most of the time at 3:37. Hannah and I will be sound asleep when all of a sudden the lights or TV will turn on. I wake up to these anomalies and realize I am not dreaming. It's not just the lights…it's also Hannah's doll. I'm worried. What do you think is wrong?"

I didn't want her to think I was a nut job, although I knew that what I was telling her made no sense at all.

Kelly looked at me with concern in her eyes and said, "I'll have the apartment handyman look around your place again when he has a chance. It sounds like there's probably still something wrong in the wiring."

I was pretty sure in that moment, she thought it was the wiring in my head.

"I would really appreciate that," I said. "I want to get to the bottom of this strange situation."

It was getting late. "I need to get back home to do the evening chores. Jessica is going to arrive soon, and I need to get dinner on the table." I thanked Kelly for the cocoa, and for listening.

As I walked back home with Hannah, I looked over to her and said, "I hope Kelly isn't on the phone calling the nut farm on me."

Hannah looked up to me and then said, "I like nuts, Mom. Almonds are my favorite."

NINE

Fried-Chicken Dinner and Ernie

When I got home, Jessica was on the couch watching TV. Hannah ran over to her and sat while I started dinner. All seemed well during the evening, but the air in the apartment was stagnant.

"Jessica, are you or Hannah hot?"

"Not really, but the air is a little dense," she said.

"I think I should open the sliding-glass door to let in the fresh air in."

"Yeah, that's a good idea, Mommy," Hannah said.

I felt a little dizzy as I stood in the kitchen making dinner. Maybe it was anxiety after the talk with Kelly, or maybe it was the anticipation of things to come. I didn't know, but I felt strange and uneasy. It had continued to rain for five straight days, and the outside air was cold, but having the glass door open made the apartment seem less dark, and for some reason, I felt a lot better with the breeze coming in.

During times of stress and discomfort, I found cooking enjoyable and relaxing. Tonight was one of those times. I decided to make a beautiful dinner for the girls and me—comfort food. Fried chicken, green beans, and mashed potatoes: a meal I had made often over the years.

The first dinner I cooked for my family, at the age of nine, was fried chicken. Hermie had a red-and-white-checkered Betty Crocker cookbook. When I was young, I read that book cover to cover, envisioning myself a young Betty Crocker. I had studied the cookbook for weeks, contemplating the perfect meal to try out my nine-year-old culinary skills. I remember I wanted to surprise my mom with dinner; she had been upset and sad since my grandfather's passing. We were all grieving.

I thought that making dinner for my mom might help ease her sadness and pain. I knew, after rummaging through the cupboards and refrigerator, that we had chicken in the freezer and some green beans from the garden. This would be the magical day my little Betty Crocker would emerge.

I had opened my cookbook to the fried chicken recipe, and I was ready to start. The cookbook said the meal would take about an hour and a half to prepare and cook. Being just nine, I decided to start at seven that morning; I wanted to make sure I had enough time for the special event.

As I was getting ready to prepare the fried-chicken meal of the century, I heard Hermie outside. When I looked, I saw her near the rabbit cages, holding the .22 caliber rifle that Grandpa had given her as a child. I wasn't sure what she was doing with her rifle. She was weeping and holding the gun in her hands as she stood next to the little rabbits. I was scared; I wondered what she was doing with the gun.

My little mind raced; my heart was beating fast. I stood there in my front doorway, observing her as she reached into the cage, pulled out one of our sweet bunnies, and wept. She held the bunny next to her heart as she stroked its head, all the while holding the rifle in her right hand. She then gently put the bunny on the ground. He started to scurry off. Hermie lifted the rifle to her chest, aimed at the little fellow, and shot him. There he lay in the dirt, dead.

Hermie cried as she set her rifle down. She walked over to the rabbit and gently picked it up. She held the dead rabbit to her chest and then slowly walked over to a wooden board that had been attached to a pine tree. She nailed the dead rabbit to the board by the ears and legs.

My little legs shook. My mouth was dry with fright. How could Hermie kill an innocent rabbit—our pet? I watched my mom as she skinned and gutted the rabbit. It was horrible. I didn't understand why she was doing this. I thought she had gone crazy…maybe over my grandpa's death three weeks before.

Shocked, I ran into the house and started cooking the meal of the century. I thought, in my child's mind, that the meal would save the day, or maybe us. I was nervous, and shaking, but I immediately got to work. My mind kept returning to the incident that had just happened. I started to cry quietly. I didn't want her to see anything out of the ordinary if she came into the house, so I stood next to the stove with my head down.

I continued to hear loud screeches outside. I was afraid to see what was going on, so I just stayed in the kitchen, working and cooking. My brothers and sister, who had been sleeping, woke up and came into the kitchen. I said, "Stay in the house. Hermie is outside acting crazy." Scared, they decided to sit in the kitchen with me.

All day, we heard rabbits screeching and gunshots echoing. We were afraid. I said to my siblings, "If we're good and cook this great meal, Hermie will be okay." I then went outside and yelled from the front porch, "Hey Hermie, don't worry about anything, I am taking care of the kids."

"Keep them in the house!" she yelled back. "I am going to be busy all day, and you're not allowed to be outside!"

My fried-chicken meal was coming along great. It took me a few tries to get things right, but the chicken was looking good, just like the pictures in the Betty Crocker cookbook. Michelle had cleaned the house and had set the dinner table. My brothers had helped with the corn and green beans from the garden. It started to get dark outside; the sky had turned gray and cloudy. Hermie was still outside in the rabbit pens. The kids and I had been inside all day working together, wondering if our mother had gone mad.

We were now dressed and cleaned up. I looked out the front door and yelled, "Hermie, we have a surprise for you." I said to the kids, "Sit at the dinner table quietly while we wait for her to come in." I was proud of our accomplishment, but the kids were restless from being inside all day. "No fighting or arguing. Be on your best behavior," I added. I didn't know how Hermie was going to react after being outside doing those horrible things to our rabbits, so I wanted everything to be as perfect as possible.

We sat quietly, staring at one another, barely moving. I heard the front door open. She walked in, her shirt and hands covered in blood. We all gasped.

"Are you okay?" I asked. She started to cry. My heart started to race, I didn't know what would happen next.

Tears poured from her eyes as she looked at the table and asked, "Is this for me, kids?"

"Yes!" I answered. "The kids and I worked on this meal all day long. We wanted to make you happy and proud."

She smiled and said, "I am going to clean up." I was relieved to see her smile. I knew the magical meal must have done the trick. When she came back to the table, she sat down in the spot we had made for her. And though she continued to have tears in her eyes, she had a smile on her face.

Together we sat to eat a lovingly prepared meal made by the hands of a little nine-year-old girl. A sense of peace and serenity filled the room. Hermie said, "I am proud of you, Jodi. I can't believe you watched the kids and made a tasty meal to boot."

I was proud of myself, too. My plan had worked; I made my mom happy. The family sat for an hour or so, laughing and talking. I told her how I had studied the red-and-white cookbook, followed the directions, and cooked this wonderful dinner.

"I am impressed," she said, "You're quite a little chef."

I was relieved. My heart and mind felt much better. However, I was still concerned about what I had witnessed earlier. I wanted to ask my mom what she had been doing to the rabbits, why she had a gun, and if she was crazy.

I mustered the strength, took a deep breath, and asked, "Hermie, what were you doing to our bunnies?"

"Jodi, Grandpa gave us these bunnies for food."

"What? What do you mean 'food'?" I asked.

I was holding what I thought was a chicken leg up to my mouth.

"We raise rabbits to eat, she said. "I kill, skin, and gut them, and then store them in the freezer."

My stomach sank and I shook, realizing that what I was about to swallow was actually one of my cute little bunnies—possibly Fluffy, whom I hadn't seen in a week.

I have to say that I will never forget my first cooking experience. I had always loved the warm comfort of foods pictured in cookbooks, but I learned to be careful when choosing the ingredients.

My mother told this story throughout my life. She would say it was one of the best meals she had ever eaten.

As I took a bite of the fried chicken—real chicken this time—a cool breeze came in from the sliding-glass door and brought me back into the present moment. I thought again about how cooking for my friends and family brought me comfort and a sense of well-being during times of stress.

As bedtime neared, I decided to ask the girls if we could pray together.

I prayed. "God, I don't understand what is going on in this apartment. Please send your guardian angels to watch over us as we sleep."

While I prayed, Hannah chimed in with a quick, "Yeah, God—send the angel with the long, brown hair. I like her."

I didn't think anything at the time, but soon her request for the long-haired angel would make sense.

After our prayer, Jessica, Hannah, and I walked into the bedroom and snuggled into my bed together. It was hard to let myself drift off to sleep; I was anxious about what might happen next. I eventually fell asleep, and before I knew it, morning had arrived without incident.

It was 7:00 a.m. We had made it a whole night without any interruption. I felt elated! It was our first uninterrupted night in a week. I hoped this was a new beginning and that the strange anomalies were over. *Thank you, God! Thank you, God!*

The following week was calm. Nothing out of the ordinary happened in the apartment. I talked to Kathy again and confirmed our arrangement for Jessica to continue to stay with me. I didn't get into any details regarding why I wanted her to stay, and she never asked, so just left it as though I hated to be alone.

The girls and I were relieved that the odd occurrences had stopped; however, worry lurked in the back of my mind. Something very intense had definitely just happened to us, so something similar could still happen.

I didn't want to jinx my good fortune by talking about what had occurred, so I kept my thoughts to myself and prayed each night before bed. Jessica continued to stay with me and attended school each day. I was now hoping the strange happenings were finally behind us, and we could go on with normal lives.

Unfortunately, things didn't remain dormant for long.

The day started out beautifully. As I looked out the sliding-glass window I could see the sun was on the horizon, lighting up the underside of the overcast sky. The clouds were a radiant golden color, and I thought to myself, "There will always be good days and bad days. I pray for this day to be a good one."

Jessica left for school, and I decided to take Hannah for a walk to Bidwell Park. I knew it was only a matter of time before we would have another rainstorm. We ended up spending the entire day at the park, playing in the sunshine. Before we knew it, it was time to get home to meet Jessica.

Walking back to the complex, I felt a strange stirring in the pit of my stomach. I was anxious, tense. A sense of impending doom lingered in the air as we neared the complex. Life had been going well for the past week. I didn't want that to change.

When I finally arrived at my apartment, I found Jessica patiently waiting outside for me, as I was the only one with a key. As Jessica, Hannah, and I walked in one by one, we saw that the apartment looked to be in perfect order, though the strange gnawing feeling continued conspicuously in the pit of my stomach. The energy seemed eerie again. Jessica sat on the couch as Hannah and I headed to my bedroom.

When I walked by Hannah's room, my throat tightened and I felt a sudden wave of panic run through my body. As I looked over to my right, I noticed the receiver to my telephone lying in the center of her room. The cord had been wrapped tightly around it. Next to the telephone sat the coveted Ernie doll—with a piece of rope wrapped around his neck.

"Jessica, come here quick!" I yelled. She ran to me. "Look—what the hell is this?"

"What? What?" she replied.

There, in the middle of the floor, lay Ernie with a noose around his neck in what looked like a staged crime scene.

"What is going on here?" asked Jessica, sounding both concerned and perplexed.

Puzzled and frightened, we looked at each other, searching for an explanation.

"Do you think this is a prank, or some kind of sick joke?" I asked Jessica. "Why do you think someone would put a rope around Hannah's doll?"

"I have no idea," she replied. "This is so strange."

As we looked around the apartment, we saw nothing missing; no windows had been opened or broken. Nothing other than the phone and Ernie doll had been tampered with. I knew Hannah couldn't have fashioned such an elaborate noose or wrapped a phone receiver so neatly. Why would someone do such a strange thing?

Calling the police crossed my mind, but what would I say to them? "Hi, Ernie is sitting in my little girl's room with a noose around his neck, and next to him on the floor is the phone receiver—oh, and the cord is neatly twisted around it." They would have told me to go to the mental hospital around the corner.

There was nothing I could do! I picked up the phone receiver to examine it. Jessica and I looked at it again and again. I was completely freaked out. Everything felt surreal.

I decided to call Jenny. She didn't answer, so I left a message: "Jenny, call me as soon as you get home. Something really strange happened. We are okay, but I'm just freaked out."

The girls and I went to the kitchen and stood there staring at each other, trying to figure out what had just happened and what to do. It had been a fine day up to this point—in fact, the entire week had gone by without anything strange happening. So what had changed?

The girls and I decided to leave the apartment. We didn't feel safe. My home had been invaded—again! By whom or what, we still didn't know.

We left the apartment, making sure to lock the door behind us. The girls and I got into my car and headed to the diner around the corner. I needed to sit for a while and think. Something freaky was going on in my apartment, but who was going to believe me? I hardly believed it my-self! At least there were witnesses, even if they were Jessica and Hannah.

I sat there with the girls in the diner, trying to make sense of nonsense. Jessica and I chatted back and forth, trying to figure things out. Neither of us wanted to go to the apartment. We weren't sure whether we should tell the manager or call the police. My savings were dwindling, so staying in a motel was out of the question. Jenny was preg-nant and had a full house, and Jessica's mom, Kathy, also had a full house. I really didn't have any other option than going back to the strange apartment.

After an hour or so at the diner, we decided we would go back and call the police. We would at least have peace of mind knowing the apartment had been looked through by a trained professional. As I sat in the diner, I felt like a warrior preparing for a battle.

We finished drinking our tea. I took a deep breath and let out a huge sigh before getting up to pay the bill.

Walking to the car, Jessica said, "Jodi, I know that we are going to be okay. There has got to be a reasonable explanation for what happened."

I really wanted to believe her. I really did. I wanted there to be a reasonable explanation for every strange anomaly that we had experienced, but what could it be?

It was dark when we pulled up to the apartment complex. I put on my warrior face, and this time, as I walked through the door, I felt a guardian angel by my side. I had a sense of peace and strength; I knew we were going to get through this turmoil.

Jessica and I went inside and called the Chico Police Department. I could tell the police dispatcher who took the call thought I was a kook as I tried to explain the incident, but I didn't care. I persisted with the explanation and insisted she send an officer to check my apartment. About an hour later, there was a loud, strong knock at my front door, and then a male voice said, "Chico Police, we are here to check on a possible break-in." I walked over and opened my front door. A tall, dark-haired man in a blue police uniform walked inside. "Hello, are you Miss Foster?" he asked. "My name is Officer Walker. I am here to take a report on a possible break in involving an Ernie doll." He smirked at me. "I am going to take a look around the apartment."

"Yes of course," I replied. "My daughter, Hannah, Jessica, and I had come home after a day at the park and school to find this unusual incident in my daughter's room, sir." He looked into Hannah's room and asked, "Miss Foster this looks like a typical little girl's room with toys. Did any of you touch anything in the room?" I said, "Actually I did sir, I picked up the phone and the Ernie doll." I could tell the officer was annoyed with me. He made the snide remark, "So Miss Foster, it looks like Ernie's been acting up. Were Bert and Elmo involved too?"

He looked around and said, "Miss Foster, it is against the law to make a false police report. I will let you off with a warning, but if this happens again, you will be in trouble."

Was he serious?

"Officer," I said, "I am afraid there is something really wrong. I didn't stage this situation. What if someone else did? What if someone is stalking me?"

I felt intimidated by his arrogant demeanor, but I persisted with the questions because I was really frightened. And for the first time, I actually thought that there might be someone in the complex trying to hurt Hannah or me.

Officer Walker shook his finger at me. "Miss Foster I have had just about enough of this storytelling. I suggest that the next time you call the police, there is a real issue, or you will be arrested!"

He turned around, walked down the hallway, and out my front door. He left without filing a report.

I felt sick to my stomach, and broken. I felt abandoned, rejected, and discriminated against. All I could do was fall to my knees and cry next to Ernie, who lay on the floor with a noose around his neck.

TEN

Childhood Reality

It was another dark and stormy night. The crescent moon gleamed through the gray clouds. There were a few white twinkling stars peeking through the rain-filled clouds, which gave a slight amount of harmony to the night sky.

A few days had passed since the incident with the Ernie doll. The air in the apartment seemed to always carry a sense of urgency, though somehow I was getting used to it. The amount of tension would ebb and flow; however, when something strange was about to occur, the energy would get static and heavy.

Around 9:00 p.m., I decided to give Hannah her bath. We were in the bathtub together, laughing and playing amid bubbles and suds, when out of the blue, Hannah said, "Mama, I like that girl that visits us."

"What girl, honey?" I asked.

"You know, Mom. The girl who walks around our house."

"What girl, Hannah?"

"Mom, she has long brown hair and green eyes. She is really nice."

I was trying to figure out what the heck she was talking about. She was only three, but quite advanced at talking. I asked her if she meant Kathy, Jessica, or Jenny; she replied no each time.

"She lived in the upstairs apartment, but sometimes she comes to visit us here, in the downstairs apartment."

Confused, I said, "Kelly, the manager?"

"No, Mama, she is different. She comes over at night, but sometimes in the day, too. You know her name—My-Belle."

I was perplexed. I didn't know who or what she was talking about, but I listened to her story.

Hannah continued. "She kissed me on the head at night when I was sleeping."

I assumed she had made up an imaginary friend. I remembered how my sister and I had made up imaginary friends on occasion when we were little, and I said to her, "When me and my sister Michelle were little, we would pretend we were girl cops, in a show called *Charlie's Angels*, and we would make up people, places, and games."

"Mama, I am not pretending. This is a real girl!" she insisted.

"Well maybe, Hannah, she's a guardian angel, visiting you in your dreams."

"No, she is real, Mama."

I didn't want to argue with a three-year-old so I changed the subject and talked about angels and my grandma. "Hey honey, did you know that my grandma came to me in a dream, to tell me about you?"

"What did she say, Mama?"

"She told me your name was going to be Hannah Rose. Do you know what your name means?"

"What, Mama?"

"'Gift from God,' honey," I replied. "You're my gift from God."

I picked up my wet, soapy child and wrapped her in a towel. I dried her off and held her close to my heart as I carried her into the bedroom.

While I lay in bed with Hannah, drifting off to sleep, I thought about dreams, angels, and spirits. How real they had seemed, so much more real as a child. After dealing with an arrogant cop, unimaginable paranormal anomalies, and nonbelief, I was starting to believe children might have more sense, acceptance, and reality than adults.

That same night, I had another dream. It was again about a location in a field 35.76 miles northeast of Red Bluff. Somehow, as I dreamt, I knew intuitively that this precise location was important. During this dream, I felt as if I were flying, as though I were a bird looking over a green pasture with lava rocks. To my right were snow-capped mountains.

After I flew for a while, I landed and found myself lying in a green field.

In front of me, I could see a big lava rock, about two-and-a-half-feet tall and four feet in length. Somehow I was behind it, lying in the green pasture, beneath the dirt. There was morning dew on the ground, and I smelled farm animals—horses and cows. I heard a stream nearby.

The dream was vivid and colorful, but I sensed something was wrong. I felt cold; I started to shiver. I needed help, but as I looked around, there was no one. I was alone.

I knew I wasn't the person in the dream. I was somebody else, but I couldn't see or understand who that person was.

When I awoke, the time was 3:37 a.m. However, this time, instead of freaking out, I grabbed a piece of paper from my nightstand and made a note regarding the details of the dream. Somehow the act of writing helped me to put things into perspective, and I was able to get back to sleep quickly.

When morning arrived, I knew in my soul, and in the pit of my stomach, after everything that occurred and the numerous dreams, that this was some kind of spiritual issue, but I still wasn't able to piece the puzzle together.

I grabbed my coat, purse, and the kids. I raced from the warm house to the cold car. As I sat in the car, letting the engine warm up, I watched the clock. By now, it was almost 7:00 a.m., so I said to the girls, "It's time to get going." I dropped Jessica off at school and headed straight over to Jenny's house. I parked my car and headed for her front door. I knocked for a minute before my friend answered the door.

"You're up early," Jenny said. "Is everything okay?"

I walked inside, sat in front of her warm heater on the floor, Hannah in my lap, and said, "Jenny, I am just going to get straight to the point—I think it might be haunted!"

Though this is what I had been thinking for some time, this was the first time in a while that I had heard myself say it out loud.

"Jodi, you're nuts!" she said, laughing.

"No, I mean it. Many, many weird, unexplainable things have happened in that apartment. I can't keep ignoring these anomalies. Something is wrong."

"Tell me what's going on," Jenny said. "Are you serious, or should I take you to the mental hospital?"

"Maybe I am nuts, but then so are Jessica, Kathy, you, and Hannah. We will need that family plan, since we've all experienced the same strange occurrences."

I started to cry and tell her about every strange anomaly, detail by detail—the dreams, everything. I told her about the phone cord incident, the mini-blinds, and the lights, and how the cops thought I was crazy. I explained how the lights and TV turned on when I turned them off, and off when I left them on during the night, and how two different Ernie dolls screamed, "I feel great! I feel great!" I couldn't keep my concern and fright inside any longer.

Jenny looked at me with concern in her eyes. "Jodi, why didn't you tell me sooner? Good God, are you okay?"

"I know this is hard to believe, but it's all true—everything." I held my head in my hands while I sat in her easy chair, shaking.

"So Hannah and Jessica have experienced all of this strangeness, too?"

"Yes! Yes!" I said. "This is why I asked Jessica to stay with me. I was scared to be alone in the apartment. I didn't want to bother you since you're pregnant."

Jenny stood in her living room, in shock.

"But I have no one to turn to," I said. "And who is going to believe me? You said your parents are from Cuba, and your grandfather was a medicine man who practiced Santería. Do you think he could help?"

"I will ask him for prayers. Cuban rituals usually involve herbs, candles, dances, and prayer," Jenny said.

Since I had been raised a Christian, when talking about living in a haunted house, I naturally thought of negative spirits or horror movies where people were sucked into the TV. "Do you think there is an evil spirit in my house?" I asked. "When I was little, my grandpa told me that there was a spiritual realm, but I basically blocked out all those childhood memories."

"This isn't my area of expertise, but I will do my best to help you figure it out," Jenny replied.

"Jenny, I really want to move, but I can't afford to."

"I will try to call my grandfather to see what he suggests we do. If there is an evil spirit in there, we will get to the bottom of this. In the meantime, you have Jessica, and now me to help you through this situation."

It was late afternoon now. Jenny and I had been talking for hours. Hannah was playing with Jenny's three-year-old son, Phillip. I could overhear them having a conversation. It was about our apartment and how sometimes Ernie would yell in the middle of the night when we were trying to sleep. Listening to them was both alarming and charming.

I heard Hannah say, "Maybe it's my guardian angel when she comes to kiss me on the head at night. I think she is the one who turns on the lights—maybe she can't see, so she turns them on. My mom told me that angels can come and visit in dreams, but she isn't in my dreams. She is real."

Hannah added, "I'm not scared. My angel is nice. She just wanted to let us to know she was there with us."

She was so matter-of-fact about things. She then turned her little head and saw me listening and said, "Mom, angels don't make things scary. It's the people who hurt angels that are scary. Here is a picture of the angel in our house, and some people she doesn't like."

She got up, walked over to me, and handed me two pictures drawn in red ink. I was startled by her drawings, which were eerily detailed and looked almost real. One was a picture of a girl who had a flip hairdo and was wearing what looked like a sweater and a pair of pants. The other picture was of three people. There was a man and a woman, both with glasses. The man had a scary look on his face and wore sideburns. They were standing next to what looked like the same girl in the other picture. She had something tied around her neck and a tear running down her face, the picture took me by surprise because they were hauntingly gruesome—the red ink resembled blood.

"Thank you, honey," I said. "These are really interesting. Why would you draw these pictures for Mommy?"

Hannah said, "My angel, My-Belle told me to. The people hurt her, Mom."

"Honey, what are you talking about, hurt her?" I asked.

"I don't know. She told me they hurt her neck," Hannah replied.

I folded them and put them in my purse. Hannah wanted me to take them home and put them on the refrigerator, but I was unsure if I really wanted these drawings hanging where I had to see them every day.

Afternoon was coming to an end and Jessica was going to be home soon, so I needed to get back to the apartment.

"Jodi, I just called my cousin the psychic a few minutes ago, and he suggested that you get some white candles and daisies for your apartment."

"What for?" I replied.

"He said that burning white candles in your environment will aid with mental clarity. White symbolizes peace, spiritual truth, and serenity; the white daisy symbolizes innocence," Jenny explained.

Jenny asked me to call her as soon as I got home. We also made plans for her to come over the following day. On the way home, I stopped at the grocery store to pick up some white candles and daisies.

I met Jessica at the front door of my apartment. Before I walked in, I lit the white candle and held tight to the flowers Jenny had given me. The kids were behind me. We made our way together through the apartment, looking into each room with the candle guiding our way. I was scared, not knowing what I might encounter. Jessica was just as nervous, although slightly intrigued by my newfound ritual. It felt funny, as if I were in a comic horror film waiting for a spook to jump out from the closet.

I wondered what a white candle or flowers would really accomplish. If I did encounter something was I supposed to throw them at it? Jenny had forgotten to explain that part. At this point, I was willing to try just about anything.

We made it through the entire apartment with me leading the way, candle in hand. Things seemed just fine. I was relieved. I continued to hold the candle, ready for attack, just in case. I think the humor of this performance brought me back to reality. I started to laugh. I was able to call Jenny and tell her we were fine. Maybe the candle-flower combination really had done the trick.

That night, before bed, I walked through the apartment with the candle and flowers again. I was determined to overcome what I was now calling a haunted apartment and paranormal activity.

Before bed, I grabbed my Bible, the flowers, and the white candle. While I lay there with the girls, I decided to look through some passages. I didn't really know what page to start on, so I prayed for direction. I opened the Bible to Philippians 4:13: "I can do all things through Christ who strengthens me." Then I turned and opened again to another passage, Matthew 7:7: "Ask and it shall be given, seek, and you will find, knock, and the door shall be opened to you." I knew I had been divinely directed to these verses.

"God, here it is, in your words," I said. "'Ask in your name, and it will be given. Seek, and I will find.' Please, Jesus, come to my rescue. Help me and Hannah. We need to feel safe. Please don't let strange things happen again! I am scared and frightened! I know you don't want me to be afraid. I am asking in your name to be freed from this haunted horror."

I must have prayed and read the Bible for two or three hours. The last words I said before falling asleep were, "God, please give me an answer. I need to know why I have experienced so many strange anomalies since moving into this apartment. Is there something evil here? What do I do if there is something evil in this apartment? Is it the devil trying to lead me astray from you, or is there more for me to understand?"

I must have cried myself to sleep, because the next thing I knew, I was waking up to my sweet child kissing me on the head.

"Mama, it's time for school. We have to wake up Jessica so she can catch the bus."

I looked over to the clock. It read 7:00 a.m. Hannah was right: It was time for school. Jenny would soon be on her way to my house. To relieve my anxiety as I waited for Jenny to arrive, I decided to take a walk outside. I grabbed Hannah and headed out the door. After standing outside in the cold for about half an hour waiting for Jenny, I decided to go back inside.

Hannah and I sat on the couch together, wrapped in a cozy blanket. About twenty minutes later, Jenny knocked on my door. Hannah rushed over and let her in. I was glad to see her and Phillip.

"I am so glad you are here. I was feeling nervous and didn't want to be alone much longer. Go ahead and make yourself at home while I make us some coffee."

I thought that a good jolt of caffeine would be just the thing to get us in the mood for a day of chatting and introspection. As we sat in the living room, I finally started to relax. Hannah and Phillip went to her room to play.

I told Jenny about how the kids and I had lit our white candle and made our way through the apartment with the flowers, praying and blessing each room. She laughed and said that must have been a funny sight to see. I agreed.

We spent the day talking and eating. After a while, Jenny got tired and asked if she could take a nap in my bedroom. I gave her a warm blanket and fluffed the pillows for her. I sent the kids to play in the living room, so she could have some quiet.

Hannah and Phillip sat on the living room floor next to me while I lay on the couch. They played with Hannah's Ernie doll and some other toys. While I watched the kids play together, I couldn't help but be a little frightened as I looked at Ernie. Ernie was the doll I'd found with a noose around his neck, and he had also been waking us up on occasion at 3:37 a.m., screaming. I wondered if I should have thrown him away a couple weeks ago. After looking at the doll awhile, I decided that it was time to send him on a long overdue vacation...but I would have to wait for the right moment so Hannah wouldn't freak out.

Listening to the kids play and laugh was good for my nerves. I was able to relax and let my mind wander, leading me to daydream about playing with my sister, Michelle. When we lived together in the mountains, we would pretend to be fairies and put on costumes and makeup together. Sometimes we were lucky enough to capture my brother Carl and talk him into letting us dress him up, too. After dressing up, we would head outside to the forest behind our house to play in our imaginary fairy world.

My sister and brothers and I were avid explorers, spending many hours searching for interesting spots in the mountains to play. One day we found an abandoned shack behind our house in the middle of the pine trees. Looking back, I think it must have been an old hunting shack. It wasn't fancy, just a tiny old structure to get out of the harsh climate if need be. When my sister and I found the shack in the middle of nowhere, we thought it was made for us, and we turned it into our fairy fort. We played there for hours together, flying around in our costumes and finding beautiful rocks, fragrant flowers, and interesting pieces of wood. We crafted dolls and other fairy goodies with all the carefully collected materials. The shack was our sanctuary—no adults were allowed to know about it.

I remember the sacred songs we would sing and verses we would say before entering our fairyland together. One verse went like this: "Only fairies, pure of soul, will be able to enter, come and go. Our sacred space is ours to play—only fairies are allowed to stay."

As I lay on my couch, reminiscing about special times as a child, I couldn't help but think that maybe we were on to something back then. We had made those sacred verses and rituals for safety—maybe as adults, we needed to do the same thing before moving into houses and apartments.

Maybe last night's candle-and-flower ritual wasn't as silly as I thought after all. Maybe it was the beginning of a new understanding.

I continued daydreaming of fairyland as the kids played and talked. I listened as they made up stories and played, just as I had done. It seemed like a perfect opportunity to share my story about fairies in the mountains. The children listened intently as I told them how I played with my sister and fairies in the pine trees. Hannah looked at me, wide-eyed, as I reminisced.

After I shared my story with the kids, Hannah said, "Mommy, I have a story about a beautiful fairy angel who lives in our house. She has long, beautiful brown hair and big, beautiful green eyes. She walks around the house looking for things to play with."

"Really, Hannah? That is so cool," I replied.

Then Hannah said, "Her name is My Belle." I felt the hair on the back of my neck stand on end, and a cool breeze drifted through the living room. I sat up to see if the sliding glass door was open. It wasn't. This was the second time she had mentioned that name in the past two days.

I lay back on the couch, listening to the kids continue their chatter. While I lay there, the conversation with Hannah in the bathtub popped into my mind. I recalled her mentioning the same name.

"Hannah, is My Belle your guardian angel?"

"Yep, Mama."

"Now, is she your angel, or a friend of mine?"

"Both," she replied, exasperated. Then she said, "Mama, can't you see her?"

I remembered saying the same thing to my mom and sister when I had encountered the Native American boy at age nine.

Could Hannah be having a similar experience?

Chills ran through my bones. "Is she here now?" My heart skipped a beat in anticipation of her reply.

"No, Mama. She is with the other angels."

I was relieved. I wasn't ready to encounter what I had experienced as a child again.

"Hannah," I said, "if you do see your angel again, please tell me." Hannah and Phillip continued to play, while I lay muddled in thought.

Before long, Jessica was home from school, Jenny was awake, and everyone was hungry.

Jenny and I prepared a yummy, home-cooked meal, and we all sat down together. My apartment had a sense of family and home. It was nice to entertain and to share good conversation and food. I thanked everyone for spending the day, and most of the night, with me. It was getting late and time for Jenny to leave.

As we said our goodnights, I said, "I will see you to-morrow."

The girls and I decided to get together before bed to do another prayer and white candle-and-flower ritual. After completing our prayer, Jessica told me she had a very important field trip in the morning. It was imperative she be at the bus stop no later than 6:30 a.m. because she was in charge of refreshments and roll call.

Due to the importance, I decided to set two alarm clocks—one battery-operated clock in the bedroom, and one electric clock in the living room, both set for 5:45 a.m. Jessica double-checked both clocks and then went off to bed. We slept together in the back bedroom. I was in the middle and had one girl on each side. Snuggled in the warm bed, we all drifted off to a peaceful night's sleep…or so I thought.

That night I experienced the most horrific, mystifying paranormal nightmare yet.

ELEVEN

The Last Night

A beautiful girl with long brown hair was hung from a hook, naked, in a basement. Her hands were tied behind her back. It looked as if she were trying to scream, and beg for her life. She couldn't, because a white cloth was shoved into her mouth and tied around the back of her neck.

I saw a man standing next to the girl. He wore blue jeans with a leather belt. I could see the back of the belt had initials. The first letter was "H." The monster was tormenting and abusing the young girl sexually, whipping and beating her while pulling hard on her mouth restraint so she couldn't breathe. The girl was beautiful; she looked like a model from the seventies.

I felt overwhelming panic during the dream. I wanted to run away and get help, but I couldn't. I didn't understand how, but I could physically feel the pain and torture he inflicted upon the poor girl. I witnessed pure evil and horror emanating from the man.

During the dream, I couldn't see the girl's face, only her profile. The man continued whipping and hurting her, laughing and saying smugly, "You know you like this, don't you? You want this. I am your master; you will be my sex slave." I saw him take the gag out of her mouth, so he could hear her response.

I heard the young lady beg for her life. "Please . . . please stop! My parents have money. I will give you anything you want."

He didn't like her answer, so he whipped her again. "Give me the right answer, or you will suffer," he replied.

The young woman screamed and cried, "Let me go—I won't tell anyone what happened."

He angrily yelled, "Your life is mine. You will do what I say!" I could see the man getting sexually aroused as the woman hung, begging for mercy. Apparently he had planned this torture for a while. She was his prize.

I was scared. I could see the girl trying to fight the evil off, but it was hopeless. I knew these might be her last moments alive. I wanted to stop the monster, but I couldn't. I prayed. I begged God to spare her. This man was an evil monster, a devil with a huge, relentless appetite for sexual torture. I wanted out of this dream, and I wanted out now! I had witnessed enough.

The whipping, choking, and other torture continued. The beautiful woman put up a good fight, thrashing about as she hung naked from the hook. She was strong-willed and determined to live through the abuse. This made the man furious.

He then got terribly out of control. "I want silence, slave!"

The girl didn't give him what he wanted. She owned her soul! This angered him so much that he pulled out a hidden pellet gun and put it to her stomach in an attempt to scare her into submission. She now fought harder. He angrily pumped the gun, pointed it, and pulled the trigger. I saw her thin body convulse with terror after being shot.

I could see bruises already forming on her throat as she cried out, "No! Please, no!" He cocked and pumped the gun again, then put it to her throat and pulled the trigger.

"Silence, slave!" he yelled, as she continued to struggle, thrash about, and fight.

Infuriated by her will to live, he took out a knife and attempted to cut out her vocal cords. Blood poured from her throat, and tears from her eyes. There was no hope at this point. I witnessed the beautiful young lady finally giving up as her body went limp, she let go, and life left her.

Realizing she was now dead, the evil monster took the opportunity to savor every sick, twisted moment. Her death was sexually exciting for him. He lingered over her lifeless body, doing unimaginable things.

I witnessed him licking fresh blood off her breasts as he slowly chewed at and bit off her right nipple. He then pulled back her head, revealing wounds made from choking her with a noose. I saw him rip out a lock of her beautiful, long, brown hair as he took a gold watch off her wrist.

These horrifying acts sickened me to the point that I wanted to vomit. I shuddered and panicked, wondering what was next.

I suddenly found myself upstairs, where a woman sat crying on a couch. She looked up and silently mouthed, "What are we going to do now?" *Can she see me?* I realized she was talking to herself, but was a part of the nightmare scenario.

I heard the man yell, "Woman, come back down here!"

She walked to the basement below. Frightened, the woman shook with fear. I walked behind her in my dream. I watched her cry; she trembled in terror, realizing what she had helped to do.

"Take this blanket," he said. "We need to wrap her in it." Together, they took the girl's body down off the hook. I observed as the couple wrapped the dead girl in a blue blanket. So much blood had splattered the area that it looked as if an animal had been slaughtered. The horrid sight didn't seem to faze the man—he was aroused. I stood as an observer, in shock, wondering what they would do next. I remember looking around the dungeon of horror during this nightmare, when, to my surprise, I saw the spirit of the girl. She was in the corner, crying.

She looked at me and said, "Help me! Call my family! I didn't mean to die."

I couldn't. It was only a dream.

After they wrapped the girl's body, the woman, who I now realized was his wife, walked back upstairs and over to the front door.

"The coast is clear," she said and then opened it. I watched as the man carried the lifeless body to a small, dirty, blue car in his driveway. He opened the door and then carelessly shoved the dead girl's body into the back seat.

The wife stood nearby, watching for cars. The wife was shaking but continued to help, going along with her husband's twisted plan. After a few minutes, they went back into the house. I saw the man open a small, wooden box and put a lock of hair and the dead girl's cut-off nipple in it. He then added blood-soaked panties, along with the knife he had used to cut her throat. He picked up the box of nightmare and pain and held it close, as though it were a treasure. I watched as he put it under the sink in his bathroom.

After hiding the box, he went outside, where his wife was now waiting in the car. He got in the driver's seat. They were on their way to bury the body. The man knew exactly where he was going; he had been there before.

Their destination was not too far from where they lived. I remember seeing a road sign that read "Highway 44," and off to the left was a small dirt road with another sign that read "A17." The dirt road ran near a stream. During this nightmare, I could see the weather was bad; snow was falling, and the ground was wet.

The man parked the dirty old car, opened the door, and got out. He reached into the back seat and pulled out a shovel. He walked over to a big lava rock in a field and started to dig. His wife stayed in the car with the dead girl's body. He dug a small, shallow hole. After the grave was dug, the couple quickly took the body out of the car, dropped it in the ground, and covered it with the earth that was to become the young girl's grave.

I was frightened as I stood observing. I wanted to help the dead girl, but I didn't know what to do. I didn't want to see any more. I was helpless, like the dead girl—yet I was alive. I suddenly realized I was having a dream and I needed to get out, to stop the nightmare.

I told myself to wake up, and as I did, I let out a blood-curdling scream.

The alarm clocks were beeping loudly, and the apartment shook as the lights flashed on and off. The Ernie doll in the closet screamed, "I feel great! I feel great!"

I tried to gather my senses, not sure if I were awake or dreaming.

"What's going on?" Jessica yelled, and then screamed, "I'm late for school!"

I looked over to the battery-operated clock. It read 6:30 a.m. The electric clock also read 6:30 a.m. I didn't know what was happening—if it was an earthquake or what. The overhead light and the lamp continued to turn off and on. All of a sudden, the mini-blinds rose up and down by themselves, and the phone cord next to the bed started swinging like a jump rope.

I grabbed Hannah up out of the bed. I didn't want to see what would happen next. We all ran down the hallway, screaming. As we ran for the front door, I looked over at the living room clocks; they, too, read six-thirty in the morning! The lights continued to flash off and on.

Once out the front door, the girls and I headed for my car. I thought we were safe, but I was wrong.

Anxiety gripped my throat as I looked down at the time. There, on the dashboard of my car, the bright blue lights of the clock read 3:37 a.m.

I shook my head, crying, and then said, "Jessica, what time does the clock say?"

"3:37 a.m., Jodi."

Somehow, during that moment, my fear and anxiety turned to anger. I mustered up the courage to walk back to the apartment. I wasn't going to stand for an invisible force taking over my home—I wanted to fight!

Jessica, Hannah, and I stood outside the apartment in our pajamas, crying. I screamed into the apartment, "Leave us alone! This is our house—leave now!" The girls were screaming it, too. I yelled, "In Jesus's name, leave my home!"

Kelly, who lived next door, opened her door and saw us outside the apartment, crying and screaming.

"Jodi, what's going on?" she said as she walked outside.

"The lights, clocks, and the doll—we all experienced it!"

"Experienced what?"

"I don't know," I yelled. "Something…paranormal! I have tried so hard to live here, but night after night, strange unexplainable anomalies continue! I can't do it anymore!" Kelly looked into our apartment to see what was going on. When she did, her little poodle ran out of her apartment and into mine. The dog started to bark and go crazy, running around inside.

Realizing this was a serious matter, Kelly immediately said, "Come inside my apartment."

When I walked into Kelly's house, I looked over at the clock. It read 3:45 a.m. The girls and I sat on the couch in my landlady's house, crying and feeling tormented. I wasn't sure how any of this could be happening. I wondered if I should call the police again, but I was afraid I would be arrested for false reporting. I cried and cried and so did the girls.

I yelled into the air, "God, please! I don't know what to do, please help us dear God, please help us!"

Kelly said, "I am going to go into the apartment and see what was going on."

I could hear the dog barking. A plethora of emotions flooded my soul: terror, hopelessness, guilt. I didn't want to go anywhere near the apartment.

The girls and I just sat in Kelly's apartment, crying, astonished and confused after what we had just experienced.

I screamed again. "God, what just happened in the apartment?"

I heard the dog continue to bark as Kelly made her way back to us. Sitting down with us, she said, "I didn't want to venture in alone. When I poked my head in, Jodi, an overhead light bulb exploded. I am not sure why. What would make my dog go crazy?"

We all sat, crying. I was afraid. I didn't know what to expect anymore.

I spilled my guts to Kelly. I told her about every strange anomaly I had encountered since moving to the apartment complex, and about the vivid, strange dreams. I cried and shook my head in disbelief as I sat there. I had worked so hard and struggled to make a home in Chico. I was now experiencing an unimaginable paranormal crisis. But would anyone really believe me, Hannah, or Jessica?

TWELVE

Who You Gonna Call? Ghostbusters!

I was angry and confused. *What do you do when your home is invaded by an unseen force? Is there a spiritual 911?* The girls and I had just experienced something extremely mind-bending. Had it only been me, I would have thought I was insane.

Things had escalated to a point where we needed real help. The dreams and paranormal activity we had experienced were now undeniable.

"Kelly, there is something wrong in that apartment—really wrong. I don't know what to do."

"This is beyond me Jodi," Kelly said. "All I can suggest is that we pray, and pray hard!"

We all sat together and I prayed. "God, give us divine intervention and direction. None of us know what to do, or where to turn. Dear God, I can't do this on my own anymore. Something is wrong and I am scared. If there is something evil in my apartment, then please give me strength and direction to know what to do."

Jessica cried, "God, I know there is an answer. Please show us."

Kelly prayed, "God, show me how I can help these frightened girls, I really have no clue what is going on in the apartment, and we need some answers."

After our praying, I could see daylight start to break. Warm beams of sunlight came through Kelly's front window, creating a diamond pattern on her living room floor. Hannah had gone to sleep next to Jessica on the couch. Jessica, Kelly, and I continued to discuss the strange circumstances of last night's anomaly.

I said to Kelly, "You told me before that you were a Christian. I know this is a strange and bizarre question, but do you believe, I mean really believe, that the apartment could be haunted?"

"Jodi, I don't know. I suppose it is possible, but why, how, and what to do if it is, is beyond me," Kelly replied. "After everything you have gone through and all the things you have shared with me, I don't think it's a good idea for you to go back. We need to get to the bottom of this. Jodi, I know you don't have any family in town, and your income is limited, I insist that you and Hannah stay with me for a few days until we can figure out what to do."

I was relieved that Kelly asked us to stay. I decided to call Jenny to let her know what had happened. The last thing she had said to me the day before was, "I will see you tomorrow." So I didn't want her showing up and wondering where I was.

When Jenny answered the phone, I said, "I don't want to freak you out, but my apartment really is haunted, and last night proved it."

Jenny listened in shock as I laid out the night in detail.

Finally, she said, "Good God Jodi, how scary. I don't know what to do. I am going to call my cousin again."

"Call me at Kelly's house. I will be staying here for a few days," I said.

After talking with Jenny, I wondered whether there was someone local who understood paranormal experiences. I recalled a scripture in the Bible: John 8:32. "And you will know the truth, and the truth will set you free." I prayed: "Dear God, I need to know the truth, about what is going on, and I know that understanding will set me free."

I grabbed the phone book. At this point, I was willing to seek any help I could get, and after the conversation with Jenny, and receiving some seemingly helpful advice from Jenny's cousin, I decided to consult a local psychic. Though I knew some of my Christian friends would not approve, something deep inside, I guess you could call it the knowingness in the pit of my stomach, knew it would be okay.

I took a deep breath and dialed a local psychic. A woman with a soft, kind voice answered. Without hesitation, I got straight to the point.

"Hi, my name is Jodi. I was wondering if you have any experience dealing with paranormal phenomenon?"

The soft, gentle voice on the other end said, "Yes, I do have experience. How can I be of assistance?"

I chronicled the events that had happened to me and my friends since moving into the apartment complex, then said, "I know this sounds really weird, but do you think my place could be haunted by an evil spirit?"

I felt my stomach sink when I heard myself ask the question. Thoughts of black magic, witches' brews, and evil spells crossed my mind. I worried that she might ask me to bite the head of a bat and dance naked around the complex. My fears were laid to rest when she answered me with direct and matter-of-fact practical advice. "If you think your house is haunted, go to the herb store and get some frankincense, myrrh, and white candles. You will need to play soothing music in the environment while you burn the herbs and candles for seven hours. Envision a white light surrounding your apartment, declare the space yours, and then send the unwanted spirits off to the white light of Christ."

The psychic added, "While I am on the phone with you, let me say a prayer for you."

I hesitated for a minute, not sure what was going to come out of the mouth of a psychic. Then she said, "Dear God, Goddess, I ask you to send Jodi peace and understanding, surround her and her family with the white light of your loving spirit. All is as it should be, amen."

I was relieved to hear that it was a simple, normal, and kind prayer. After she was done praying she said, "I will pray and light a white candle for you. If you have any more questions, or need any other help, give me a call." I thanked the nice woman and said I would call if I needed anything. I felt a sense of peace and calmness after our conversation, but I still wasn't sure of what was really going on.

My next call, after the psychic, was to the neighborhood church. I couldn't help but wonder what kind of advice they would give me about living in what I now considered to be my haunted home.

I wonder how the advice from the church might differ from what Jenny's cousin and the local psychic suggested.

I dialed the number, and an older-sounding lady answered the phone. Nervously, I said, "Hi, my name is Jodi. I know this is going to sound completely crazy, but I think my apartment might be haunted."

The woman on the other end, who surely thought I was nuts, said, "Excuse me ma'am, but did I hear you right, you said that you're living in a haunted house? Is this some kind of joke, because I am really busy and don't have time for prank phone calls."

I took a deep breath and firmly said, "This is not a joke. My family and I have been experiencing some kind of paranormal activity ever since moving into a complex here in Chico. We have been here for about three months and the activity is escalating. Something terrible happened last night, and I really need some spiritual advice!"

I explained what had been going on, from the first day I moved into the apartment complex. I told her about my horrible dreams and noted that I wasn't the only witness to such activity—Jessica, Hannah, and two of my friends had also experienced paranormal activity.

At first, she probably thought that if this wasn't a prank call, I was probably some kind of mental patient, based on the silence on the other end of the phone. Nonetheless, I felt thankful that she didn't hang up on me before I finished my story. After I finished, she said, "I think it's best if we start out with prayer." After she prayed for me, she replied, "This subject is a little beyond my abilities, Miss Foster. I think it is best if I consult with a senior pastor. Let me get your phone number and I will give you a call later in the day."

After hanging up, I wondered if she really would have someone call me.

I sat in Kelly's living room, unable to relax. Hannah and Jessica were peacefully sleeping on the couch next to me as I waited for some kind of supernatural intervention.

After the previous night's chaos, I had completely forgotten about Jessica's field trip. We had obviously missed the bus. I called her school and said we were sick. I didn't like lying, but what was I supposed to do—tell them a ghost changed the clocks and was haunting my apartment? Throughout all the chaos, I had forgotten to call Jessica's mom to let her know what had happened. I wasn't sure how to approach the subject, but she did experience the anomaly with her keys, and jokingly suggested my apartment might be haunted. I quietly prayed that she would understand, and forgive me for letting something so unthinkable happen to her child.

Next door was the den of horror. All I could think about was how my home and sanctuary had been taken over by an unseen, paranormal energy. It was a surreal nightmare for the next few hours, as I patiently waited for a phone call from the church.

THIRTEEN

A Call from the Neighborhood Church

It was mostly cloudy out as I sat on Kelly's living room couch, looking out her window, watching the gray clouds fill the afternoon sky. It was about 2:30 when suddenly the phone rang.

The comforting warmth of the girls, who had been lying next to me sleeping, coupled with the lingering sun peering through the window, made getting up to answer difficult. My heart jumped into my throat, and my pulse raced as I anxiously walked over to pick up the phone, hoping it was the call I had been awaiting.

My voice shook, as I answered, and my mouth and throat went dry. Since it was Kelly's house, I answered by saying, "Hello, thanks for calling, Jodi speaking." I sounded like a receptionist. I heard a strong, commanding male voice on the other end say, "Hello, my name is Pastor Eric. I had an interesting message earlier regarding a possible paranormal phenomena, are you the caller?"

I was relieved to have a real pastor on the phone. I broke down crying. Through tears and panic I reluctantly said after clearing my throat, "Yes Pastor Eric, it was me that called. I know that the message I left with the receptionist sounded strange, and believe me I know it is, but I assure you that my call was not a prank, and what my family, friends, and I have been experiencing is of a serious and terrorizing nature!"

I continued, "My daughter Hannah and I moved into the apartment complex about three months ago. Upon moving in, I immediately started experiencing terrible nightmares of abduction and torture. Things mysteriously moved around in the apartment or would go missing, later to reappear in a completely different location. Lights go off and on by themselves, and for no apparent reason, my daughter's Ernie doll repeatedly goes off at 3:37 in the morning. The management had everything looked at and it all checks out to be mechanically and electrically fine."

After I finished my plea for help, I waited for a response, but all I heard was silence on the other end, and then a "Wow! Sounds like it could be an evil spirit trying to attack you and your family. I have never dealt with something of this nature. If it's all right with you

Jodi, before you go any further, I would like to do a background assessment regarding your spiritual beliefs."

"Sure, that would be fine," I replied with a slight hesitation in my voice. "Well, I believe in God and the Holy Spirit. I was raised as a Christian, and I pray." I recounted my unusual childhood, and how I moved out of my mom's house as a teen—and again as an adult when my mother had kicked Hannah and me out into the Montana snow.

After listening to me, he said, "There is probably something diabolical going on here. I will be consulting with a senior pastor named Joe, and after we talk, I will give you a call to see how we might be able to help you. Before we hang up, I would like to pray with you for protection and peace."

"Yes thank you." I cried. "I really would appreciate that Pastor Eric, since everything has been so terrifying and unnerving."

"Father God, I ask you to send guarding angels to surround Jodi, her friends, and family. Give her peace and understanding and protection, amen.

"Jodi, I will be in touch with you as soon as possible, if you need anything please feel free to give me a call. I will continue to pray, and hopefully I will have some answers for you soon."

When we hung up I felt terrified and apprehensive. I hoped that eventually all the pieces of the mysterious puzzle would fall into place. But until then, I decided to embrace the confusion, knowing inside my soul, that everything happens for a reason.

Kelly, now at work, was on her own mission. She called upper management regarding the apartment complex's history to try and find out if any other tenants had ever experienced paranormal activity.

I was anxiously pacing the floor as the girls continued to lie on the couch; they were now watching TV. I kept trying to figure out how and why this was happening.

While pacing and trying to think through the situation, I thought back to my childhood when I had experienced things that could be considered paranormal. Children don't question reality; they just experience the moment they are in as exactly that. When you're a child, days melt into one another, and dreams are real. It's as though there is no such thing as time. Children believe that what they are told is reality. Maybe there was a reason God instructed us to become like children.

I prayed: "God, please open my heart to the truth. I lay aside my preconceived notions. I choose to become like a child, and I give you permission to work with my heart and soul. As a child, I witnessed an Indian spirit boy and the spirit of a mother visiting her child in a cemetery. Both of my grandparents visited me upon their passing. I know my fear has stopped me from understanding this situation as an adult, but I want to know…I truly want an answer."

After my prayer, I sat at Kelly's kitchen table, trying to remember every detail of my experiences in that apartment. The first significant thing I recalled was the date I had moved downstairs: February 1, 2000. *The date must be significant, but why?* Looking back, I recalled that most of the paranormal activity had happened between 2:00 and 6:30 a.m., with numerous dreams and other mysterious circumstances occurring at 3:37 a.m. on the dot. I thought this, too, must be significant. I was determined to put rhyme and reason to the activity.

Kelly, now home for lunch, asked, "Did you have any success contacting anyone?"

"I had a conversation with a pastor named Eric from the neighborhood church, and was told he would consult a senior pastor who would be calling sometime today. Were you able to find anything out about the complex?"

Kelly hadn't worked for the company very long, so she wasn't familiar with its history or other tenants. "I haven't found out anything, but I am going to continue investigating this afternoon. I want there to be a reasonable explanation, but in my soul, I feel something is wrong," Kelly said.

At this point, we were in a holding pattern, waiting for some kind of resolution. Kelly went back to work, and I awaited the call.

At around 4:00 p.m., Pastor Eric called me back. I was relieved to hear his voice. It had a resounding strength and calmness.

"Hello, Jodi. Sorry it took me so long to get back to you. I had to consult with a few elders in the church to see how we could help you," Eric said.

I couldn't wait to hear what advice he would offer.

"My colleagues and I talked," Eric continued, "and we think a team of prayer warriors should come to the apartment, assess the situation, and do a prayer and music intervention. It would be best to do this during the evening if possible."

At that point, I was certainly willing to try just about anything. And again, the information I was being given closely resembled the psychic's advice and that of Jenny's Cuban relatives.

"Is it possible for you to stay anywhere other than the apartment for a few days?" he asked.

"My next-door neighbor, Kelly, who is also the manager, is letting me stay with her for the time being."

Pastor Eric agreed. "I think that is best, considering the circumstances." He also asked, "Have you had a mental-health evaluation or a physical?"

"I have an appointment set up for next month at the local county's mental-health program. I wish it were sooner, but unfortunately that was as soon as I could get in."

"After talking with you, praying, and consulting with some Christian elders, I believe you're telling the truth. You did the right thing by calling. I have a few things to ask of you. One, avoid going into the apartment alone. If you have to go in, ask a friend to go with you; that way, you will have two eyewitness accounts should any paranormal activity occur. Second thing: continue to stay with Kelly until we can come out. It might be a couple of days before I can gather everyone together. I realize this is an emergency, so here is my phone number in case the situation becomes more dire."

"Thank you for believing in my experience," I said. "I appreciate your willingness to help me, I really don't know what to say except thank you, thank you and God bless!"

"I will get in touch as soon as I can," he said.

When Kelly got home at day's end, she sat with me at her table.

"Pastor Eric called me back," I said. "He said he would come out in a couple of days to do a prayer vigil. He told me to stay at a friend's house until he could get out to the apartment."

"You and Hannah are welcome to stay here until we get to the bottom of the anomalies," Kelly said, before bringing up a new development. "While at work, I did some research about the apartment complex. I found out it was built in the late 1960s, and rumors have circulated over the years regarding strange happenings. From what I understand, there had been alleged paranormal activity in a few other units as well as the unit you're in now. The anomalies started sometime in the mid- to late seventies. Apparently a family had lived in your unit for several years, and one of their young boys told people around the complex that it was haunted."

I felt a little sigh of relief when Kelly mentioned that someone else thought it might be haunted, even if it was a child. It was okay with me because I had been thinking something similar regarding childhood beliefs, so this was a small reminder in the moment.

"What about the tenants who lived here right before me and Hannah? Did they move out for similar reasons?"

"I don't know. I was told nothing. They just up and left in the middle of the night. They had paid their rent and we didn't have any problems with them, so it is a mystery."

I had a sneaking suspicion that it might have had to do with something similar to what I was going through.

By now I was exhausted, and after being at Kelly's for the past few hours, I was feeling a sense of peace. My body and mind were finally able to relax. I knew that guardian angels, God, my friends, and the neighborhood church were looking after us.

"Do you think I could sleep on your couch tonight?" I asked.

"Of course," Kelly replied, "you have been through a lot. Get some sleep, and we will continue this conversation in the morning."

Jessica, who'd just started stirring after her unplanned nap, looked like she'd also had enough excitement for a while. "Jodi, I think I am going to call my mom. I need to get some rest and feel at peace."

"Of course, honey. I totally understand. We have both been through so much," I replied. "Have your mom come and get you."

When Kathy picked Jessica up, I told her about everything that had happened. By the look on her face, I could tell she thought I was joking. But Jessica chimed in: "Mom, Jodi is serious. Something weird has been going on, and I saw it too! We are not joking or making any of this up."

"Oh my God!" she said. "So you're really serious? What you're telling me really happened?"

I broke down and cried. "Yes! Yes! I am so sorry I didn't know what was going on, I didn't mean to expose Jessica to such strangeness."

Kathy held my hand, "I know you Jodi! Of course you wouldn't intentionally hurt Jessica. You will be in my heart and prayers. I am going to take Jessica home to rest, but I will call later to check in." We all hugged and said our goodnights.

That night I fell asleep effortlessly. I slept as I hadn't slept for months, holding Hannah next to me. I felt that the prayers from the church, the psychic, Jenny, Kelly, and I were all working to create a safe and peaceful space to rest. And I knew this was all in the hands of God now.

When morning arrived, I realized I had experienced, for the first time in a long time, a full uninterrupted night's rest. I looked out the window at the beautiful sun shining brightly. Somehow, I knew today was going to bring answers and peace.

Hannah stood up and walked to the window, and we both looked out together. She looked up at me and said, "Mama, I love you so much! My angel didn't wake us up at Kelly's house."

"No, honey, she didn't. We got to sleep through the whole night and feel safe."

"I am always safe, Mom," she replied. "You and my angel are here to watch over me."

When Hannah said that, a tear fell down my cheek. It made me feel lucky to have such a beautiful daughter. I picked her up and held her on my hip. She looked so cute in her pink pajamas and two tiny pigtails. I kissed her on the head as we stood there, looking at the sun. It was a beautiful moment.

Forty-eight hours had elapsed since we had escaped the nightmare, running out of the house in terror. The thought of going into my apartment was unbearable, but I couldn't stay in my PJs forever. I started to cry. I wanted the nightmare behind me; I wanted my apartment back; and I wanted to go home and feel safe, but we couldn't.

Kelly woke up and saw us standing at the window, crying.

"Are you okay?" she asked.

"No. I slept really good last night, but I'm crying because I need to go into the apartment to get some things for the day. Pastor Eric asked me to stay away if possible, but we need some things to get by. Maybe I should go out and buy new clothes, but my savings are dwindling."

"I have some work to do in the office," Kelly said, "but at around 1:00 p.m., we could go into the apartment and get your things together."

"Thank you, Kelly. I really appreciate of all your kindness. I don't know what I would do if it weren't for your help."

Kelly got ready for work while Hannah and I sat at the kitchen table, eating oatmeal and drinking warm tea. After being in the house for two days, I was feeling stir-crazy.

"After you go to work," I told Kelly, "I think I will venture outside to get some fresh air and sunshine."

"That would probably do you some good," Kelly replied. "I will see you around lunch."

After Kelly left, I combed Hannah's little pigtails, borrowed some lipstick and a hair clip from Kelly, and then headed out the front door. The warm sun hit my face as I walked outside, putting my nerves at ease. Something in the air seemed to give me hope that today might hold a resolution to my strange dilemma.

I walked around the complex, making sure to steer clear of my apartment, and then headed over to the pool in the middle of the complex. I walked inside and sat on a lawn chair next to the pool with Hannah on my lap. With the sun beating down on my face, I was finally able to let out a sigh of relief and breathe for a few minutes.

We must have sat there for a good hour in the sun, relaxing. After a while, I wondered what time it was. *It must be close to noon*, I thought. I noticed a few people bustling around, coming and going. I figured it must be around lunchtime. Kelly would return home in only an hour or so, and I would have to face my fear and deal with going into the haunted apartment. I sat for a few minutes, thinking about what might lie ahead. My mind wandered to horrible movies I had seen, and I wondered if any were based in reality. I thought, *What is reality? Were my childhood experiences reality? Were my adult experiences reality? Are prayers and rituals reality? Do they make a difference? The prayers I had felt over the past few days felt like they were helping.*

I continued to sit in the sun with Hannah on my lap as Hannah sang a sweet little tune. *She has such a wonderful voice; the song she's singing is actually in tune.* I started to cry uncontrollably as I listened to my daughter's innocent sweet voice.

My grandmother had told me Hannah was a gift from God, and here I was, unintentionally exposing my innocent child to frightening paranormal activities. *Will we get through this? Is there a reasonable answer, or am I insane?*

While I sat at the poolside, crying, I noticed Fred, one of the old-time renters, walking toward me. I tried to cover my face; I didn't want him to see me crying.

"How are you this fine, sunshiny day?" he asked.

My attempt at hiding my face didn't work. Unfortunately, he heard my sobs and could see that I had been crying.

"Are you okay?" Fred asked.

My voice cracked as I said, "Well Fred, no, I'm not doing very well today, I am sorry you have to see me like this."

"No worries, honey. Is it boyfriend troubles? You youngsters are always having relationship issues these days."

"I wish it were that easy, Fred, but it's a little more complicated. Things just haven't been going well for me since moving to the complex, and especially since moving to the downstairs apartment."

"Why, honey? What's going on?"

Now, at this point, I wanted to blurt out, "I am crying because...I am pretty sure my apartment is haunted!" However, I was reluctant to reveal my dilemma for fear he might run straight for the phone to call the mental hospital.

With swollen, red eyes and a pale face, I said, "The apartment wasn't as welcoming as I'd hoped it would be."

With reluctance in his voice, Fred said, "Now, honey, don't you worry."

I could sense he wanted to tell me something; I could feel the tension building as he stood there.

"I want to share a story with you about the apartment complex," Fred said, "specifically, the units you have lived in."

My mind and heart started to race; my throat started to tighten; I felt dizzy, and I wanted to flee in a panic. I wasn't sure if I could hear what he had to say, or if I really wanted too.

He then said, "Honey, no one lives in those apartments for very long, especially in the apartments located on the north end of the complex."

"Really, why?" I asked loudly. "Why, Fred?"

"This complex is where the beginning of a most bizarre occurrence happened."

"What do you mean, bizarre occurrence?" I yelled.

"Sometime back in 1976, a young college woman went missing," Fred replied. "Apparently, a couple from Red Bluff had abducted her and then kept her in a coffin under their bed—alive—for seven years. The story made the national news sometime back in the eighties."

I was in total shock as I sat in terror, listening to the crazy story. I could hardly breathe or wrap my mind around what he was saying.

"Fred, how does this story relate to me? Please! Please! I don't understand," I cried.

"I am old, so it's hard for me to remember the exact details, but to the best of my knowledge, it goes something like this: a couple from Red Bluff came to Chico looking for a sex slave. Their mission was successful, and they captured a woman."

Shaking, I yelled at Fred, "What does this have to do with my apartment?"

"Honey, their first victim lived in your apartment."

FOURTEEN

Rumors

W hat do you mean, first victim? There was more than one victim? What are you telling me? What happened to the girl who lived in my apartment? Who is she? Where is she?"

"I don't know," Fred replied. "That is all I can remember."

I didn't know if the couple was still around, searching for other victims. Was I next? Sheer panic ran through my bones. Is this the reason strange things happened in my apartment? Is there a stalker in the neighborhood?

I didn't understand how this related to an unseen force. Was God trying to tell me something?

I stood up from my chair, shaking and trembling. I grabbed Hannah and ran right past Fred and over to Kelly's office as fast as I could.

"Kelly, maybe there is an answer!" I shouted. "Maybe there is a reason for what has happened in my apartment!"

Poor Kelly sat in her office chair, staring at me with wide eyes as I shouted. I was pretty sure she thought I had gone completely mad. I was in shock, not realizing I had left Fred standing alone by the pool.

"Oh, my God, Kelly. You're not going to believe it— there might be an answer! There might be a real answer to what is happening! I will be right back with Fred."

I left Hannah with Kelly as I ran back to Fred, grabbed his hand, and said, "Come with me. Please tell Kelly what you told me." Frantically, I pulled him with me as we ran back to the office.

At the office, Fred told a story neither Kelly nor I could believe. It had made national news in the eighties. He told about a missing girl, a sex slave, and a couple who lived in a town not so far away called Red Bluff. I couldn't believe my ears. *Can I finally put rhyme and reason to all the paranormal activities?*

"Fred, are you telling me throughout the years that strange things have occurred in this complex?" Kelly asked.

"I have lived here over twenty years," Fred said, "and I have heard many strange rumors about this complex, especially a few specific units. I myself haven't had anything out of the ordinary happen, but some tenants over the years say they experienced what they called a haunting."

"A haunting?" Kelly replied. "Are you serious? This is unbelievable!"

I had to know more. "What happened to the girl? Was she found? Did the couple go to jail? Where are they now?"

"I think they are in prison, but I can't remember anything else," Fred said.

I didn't understand how such strange paranormal activity could result from this story. I was trying to wrap my mind around our newfound information.

"Kelly, maybe I should call Pastor Eric and let him know what we found out."

"Yeah, it couldn't hurt to let him know."

I grabbed the office phone and rang the church. There was no answer, but I left a voice message to call me as soon as possible. I explained on the message how over the years tenants had claimed that the complex was haunted. I knew I sounded nuts, but the embarrassment was worth it if I could get an answer and take my apartment back from the unseen force.

A few hours passed as Kelly, Fred, and I talked in her office. We had talked about the incident for so long that it was starting to get dark. I realized I was still in my pajamas and that I still needed to venture into my apartment. As interesting as Fred's historical account was, it didn't make going into the apartment any easier. I asked,

"Kelly, I need still need to get some things. Are you still willing to go with me into the unit?"

"Yes, sweetie, I haven't forgotten," she replied.

By 6:00 p.m., it was completely dark outside. We walked together from her office over to the front door of my apartment. I couldn't help but feel complete panic as thoughts regarding my last night there crept into my frightened mind. She had brought her precious little poodle along with us. We stood frightened, stalling and fearful of what might lurk inside.

I looked over at Kelly, took a deep breath, and said, "It's been three days since my last paranormal adventure."

I grabbed Kelly's hand, unlocked the door, and we both stepped into the front room of the apartment together. As we stood in the living room, my legs started to shake, and I felt a wave of panic rush over me. I wanted to turn and run out the front door, never to return, but I couldn't. I needed our things.

Kelly could see how nervous I was. She reached over to hug me and said, "You're fine. I am here with you, and we will do this together. God and guardian angels are watching over us."

After she said that, I let out a sigh and said to myself, *I will be okay.*

I looked around the living room and next to the front door, where I kept shoes and bags stacked neatly. I noticed Hannah's little pink shoes were still sitting next to mine on the floor. Everything was exactly how we had left it the night we ran out the front door screaming.

I mustered the courage to walk down the hallway to my bedroom. Unfortunately, I felt the hair on the back of my neck stand on end, and a strange tension loomed throughout the environment.

"Kelly, I'm feeling weird. Are you?"

Kelly, still standing in the living room, said, "A little, but it's probably the fact that we just finished talking with Fred and found out so much today."

I knew my feeling was something more than lingering emotion. I had taken in a deep breath and proceeded to round the corner to my room when all of a sudden, Kelly's poodle jumped out of her arms and ran past me, barking. My heart jumped out of my chest, and I started to panic. I started to turn to run back to Kelly, but as I did she proceeded to run past me down the hall after her dog. I turned and ran behind her. As she rounded the corner into the bedroom she screamed: "Oh my God! No! No!"

I thought she was yelling at the dog but then she yelled, "Oh, my God, what's going on in here!"

I rushed to her side to see what was wrong.

The dog was running around the room, barking, as Kelly and I both watched the cord to my lamp swing in midair like a jump rope.

"What is happening?" Kelly screamed.

The dog continued to bark.

We both stood there, frozen in complete shock and panic.

Somehow, Hannah's pink shoes, which had just been next to the front door, were now sitting smack dab in the middle of my bed, staring up at me. When I blinked, they had moved to the end of the bed and were pointed directly toward Kelly and me.

There was no explanation for this...absolutely none.

My mind was frozen, as were my feet. I couldn't move.

Finally, I cried, "Let's get out of here!" The dog continued to run around the bedroom, barking, as the cord swung.

Can this truly be happening? I asked myself.

But I knew it was happening, because Kelly was there witnessing the strange anomaly as well, and screaming with fright. We both continued to stand frozen with panic.

Kelly finally broke the spell by reaching over to the shoes on the end of the bed, grabbing them, reaching over to me, grabbing my hand, and pulling me out the front door as we both screamed together. We left the poor little poodle in the apartment alone, barking in the back bedroom. Once we were outside, shaking and freaked out, the dog ran out after us.

The front door to my apartment slammed shut by itself after the poodle ran out.

Kelly screamed, "I wouldn't believe it had I not been here with you and seen this with my own two eyes, Jodi! Good God above, that apartment is haunted!"

We both ran back into Kelly's house and cried together.

"I am going to call Pastor Eric right now." Kelly shook her head and cried. "The church needs to know that this is truly an emergency! Jodi, you can't go back into that place again. It's too strange and evil!"

Kelly called the main property office in Paradise, California, which was about a twenty-minute drive away, to tell them what had happened to both of us.

I heard her say, "Judy, my next call will be to the neighborhood church. We need an emergency intervention. We are all Christians here, so let's start a prayer chain. Call everyone you know to pray for the complex."

Before I knew it, Kelly was on the phone with Pastor Eric, explaining the extreme emergency and telling him that he needed to bring out his team of people that night, if possible. I listened as Kelly frantically organized this spiritual intervention. She was like a warrior getting ready for battle. She was a spiritual inspiration to me, because though she was scared out of her wits, she seemed to have a handle on the situation.

That evening, at around ten, there came a knock at Kelly's door. When I answered, a tall, round man with a balding head and a tidy beard greeted me with, "Hello, my name is Pastor Eric. You must be Kelly."

"Actually, I am Jodi," I said. "Please, come in. Thank you so much for taking the time to help us; you can't even imagine how terrorized we feel."

Walking in behind him were about four others, whom he introduced as the youth ministry. They had guitars and Bibles in tow.

Kelly came out from her bedroom and said, "Nice to meet you. Please, please sit down!"

They sat down with us at the kitchen table. I was so nervous and exhausted; the past few days were like nothing I had ever experienced—ever!

Pastor Eric didn't waste any time. He got right to the point: "Jodi I need to ask you some questions about your family's spiritual history."

"Sure Pastor Eric, whatever we need to do," I said.

I closed my eyes, hung my head, and cried. "Pastor Eric, I feel so stressed out and tired. I am afraid to tell you about my dysfunctional family. It's not good. My mom is an alcoholic. Like I told you a few days ago, I was living in Montana with her when she decided to kick us out into the snow. It was horrible; I stayed in a small cabin and worked hard to move back here to Chico. And now here I am...in an apartment that is no longer my home. It's a den of terror and fright."

I continued to weep. "I feel like it's somehow my fault. Please, I am so sorry. Please help me. Please help!"

Kelly got up and walked over to me. "Jodi, honey, it's not your fault. We are actually doing something positive here. Keep the faith. Something good will happen; I know it."

Pastor Eric said, "We are all here to help, not to condemn you and your family, honey. I just wanted to assess the situation, so we can better assist you with your home."

"I am a Christian," I said. "I was taught that if you call on the name of Jesus that evil had to vanish. I prayed in the name of Jesus, and read the Bible. Why didn't it stop? Why? Did I do something wrong?"

Pastor Eric replied, "There is strength in numbers, Jodi. God's word says that when two or more are gathered in his name, they can move mountains."

On that note, we all sat and prayed for God to intervene and reveal answers to why my apartment was haunted.

After the prayer, I said, "I have some interesting information regarding the history of the unit. Fred, who has lived here for over twenty years, said there was a girl who had lived at the complex who went missing sometime back in the mid-seventies. Maybe she is connected to the paranormal activity."

"I don't think that's the case," Pastor Eric replied, "but we will pray for the missing girl anyway."

I felt disappointed that he didn't draw the same conclusion as Kelly and I had. But I didn't want to say anything, since he was trying to help me.

The whole team sat in Kelly's apartment, praying with fervor. I was hoping for a miraculous, life-altering occurrence.

After we finished praying, the team walked over to my apartment. Pastor Eric opened the front door, walked in, and sat in the middle of the living room. The rest of the team followed. I stood in the doorway, frightened. I was waiting for something to happen.

I heard Pastor Eric say in a strong, resounding, authoritative voice, "Father God, we are here on behalf of this young woman and her family. We ask for your holy blood to wash away all evil and sin that exists in the apartment. Bring this young woman peace of mind and soul. We re-dedicate Jodi's home, soul, and child, Hannah, to you."

The others chimed in with prayers like, "Yes, Jesus. Yes, Lord. Help this woman; she is your child." They played their guitars and sang in unison, "Father, we adore you; we lay our lives and that of Jodi before you."

I waited for something terrifying to happen; my thoughts wandered to horror films like *The Exorcist* and *The Amityville Horror*. I wondered if someone would levitate or implode. *Will the lights flash off and on? Will someone run out screaming?* I was ready for anything at that point, but nothing happened. Slightly disappointed, I wondered, *Why does everything seem calm now when Kelly, Hannah, Jessica, and I experienced so much paranormal activity?* After a few minutes of standing in the doorway, I decided to go back next door to wait for the diagnosis.

I could hear Pastor Eric and his team continuing to sing and pray. They prayed throughout the entire night. When daylight broke, I realized that I had lain on Kelly's couch, with Hannah, for the duration. I had been in a trancelike state as I listened to the continual music and prayer.

I thought that prayer and music have been used in all religions and cultures to make a change. People dance and chant to celebrate or mourn in observance. There is a real quality of communion between the physical and the spiritual to these acts that, as adults, we tend to forget. Children, however, remember more often to dance, sing, and pray.

Was it as simple as remembering again?

Kelly walked into the living room and said, "Good morning. I hope you had a peaceful night's rest."

I was suddenly brought back to the moment, aware that the music had stopped.

"I didn't really sleep much," I said. "I was anticipating something horrible happening. I hope the prayer vigil worked. Unfortunately, something in my soul tells me it's not over yet."

"Jodi, it's over!" Kelly said. "God works in mysterious ways; we did the right thing by having the church come out. Many, many people are praying about the situation. It's going to be okay. Evil won't win!"

"Is what happened in my apartment—evil? Do you really think it's the devil, or related to my family's past sins? What about what Fred said?"

"I don't have an answer, but I know prayer works," she replied.

"Thank you for being here for Hannah and me. I don't know what I would have done without you. I don't want to seem ungrateful or unappreciative. Everything has been so weird."

Within minutes of our conversation, there was a knock at the door. It was Pastor Eric.

"Ladies, I just wanted to let you know that we're leaving. I am sure that whatever was interfering with your lives has been taken care of. I am confident things will be back to normal. If you need anything at all, please feel free to call. I will check in with you in a couple of days."

Kelly and I thanked everyone for all their kindness and help. And I was pleasantly surprised to hear that no one had levitated, imploded, or went running out of the apartment screaming. No one had experienced any paranormal activity at all during the vigil, which I thought was extremely strange considering that everyone else who had been there had.

The next few days were a blur; everything was surreal. So many things had happened over the past weeks. That, and the lack of sleep, had me weary. Although the apartment was now supposed to be fine, I still wasn't sure. I wasn't ready to go back even though it had been prayed for and blessed. I trusted Pastor Eric and his team of warriors. However, some things were still a mystery to me. I felt I needed some distance from the space to figure out why I personally had experienced so many nightmares and so much paranormal activity. Hannah and I continued to stay with Kelly. She knew I wanted to move far away from the complex, and she came to me with an interesting offer.

"The management company is willing to move you to one of their other complexes in downtown Chico. They are willing to pay for your move; however, there is one condition. You can't tell anyone about the paranormal activity you experienced."

Kelly added, "Honey, I am being transferred to a complex about an hour south of Chico in two weeks. Why don't you take their offer and put this nightmare behind you?"

I truly wanted the haunted-apartment incident to be a mere memory, something to put in the back of my mind and never revisit, so I accepted the gracious offer and moved without hesitation.

I thought that in moving, my haunted adventure would soon be over. Little did I know that my spiritual journey had barely begun.

FIFTEEN

Signs and Signals

The sun was shining and a soft breeze was lightly blowing from my open bedroom window. The sound of a lawn mower was humming in the background. The scent of wildflowers lingered in the air. I set my automatic coffee maker for 8:30 a.m., and I smelled the aroma of freshly brewed coffee calling me.

Spring had sprung and Hannah and I were living in our new apartment on Salem Street in downtown Chico. I was elated and I felt as if I had finally come home.

Before moving in to my new downtown home, I took spiritual precautions. I did my own little ritual and blessed my new home with white candles, flowers, prayer, and music.

I was focused on making a happy environment for myself and Hannah. I was finally settled into our home, rested. I hadn't had such peace of mind in a long time. Since the weather was exceptionally good, I decided it was time to venture out and around downtown Chico.

It was mid-May, warm and beautiful outside. I decided to put Hannah in her stroller and cruise around downtown. I didn't know many people at that time, so I enjoyed meeting the locals at different coffeehouses and bookstores.

One day as I sat at my favorite coffee shop, enjoying some tea with Hannah, I met a local old-timer named Hank. He was in his late seventies, a tiny man with gray hair and a black fedora that made him look as if he were still living in the forties. Hank was a friendly man who had lived in Chico his entire life. Sitting with Hannah, I would listen to him and his friends talking about local government and how things had been better back in the good old days. Apparently, Hank had worked in local government in his younger years and, from what I could tell, knew just about everyone in and around Chico. He was now retired and spent most of his time chatting with his buddies about fishing and hunting, and how things used to be much quieter back in the good old days.

Hank was a funny old guy. One early morning we struck up a conversation. We talked about where I was from and how I had recently moved from Montana to Chico. I told him that I had lived here before when my grandmother was sick with cancer. I had missed Chico and wanted to come back. I told him I had moved to an apartment nearby and was really enjoying it. Hank talked about how nice Chico was for starting a family. He'd raised his kids there, and his grandkids lived there as well. Hank's wife was terminally ill, but would let him go visit his friends each day for a couple of hours. Afterward, he would go home and sit with her while the nurses tended to her.

I was glad to have met Hank that morning. Chico was once again feeling like the place I remembered it to be.

When I got home from my downtown adventure with Hannah, I was tired, so I decided to take a nap. It was after lunch, and Hannah was getting tired, too. We lay down together for a little rest, and I drifted off to sleep.

During this nap, I had a dream. It was mysterious, but not scary.

There was a woman who looked as though she were in her forties. She wore round glasses and dowdy clothing. Her hair was light brown with blond highlights. She didn't look striking in any way—the kind of woman who you could pass in the street without noticing. She was sitting on a chair behind a desk doing paperwork. She appeared to be in a doctor's office. I observed her writing things down on a notepad. She talked to people as they came through a glass door and sat down in front of her. In the dream, she seemed detached and distant as she assessed and talked to these people.

Upon closer examination, I noticed it was a counseling office. This woman was talking to distressed people about their problems. I thought it strange, because she wasn't engaging or friendly as she talked with people who were obviously distraught. She walked back and forth, talking to people but never looking up or directly into their eyes. She had a cold and uncomfortable way about her, and I felt put off by her demeanor.

When I woke up, I got out a notepad and wrote a note to myself about this odd woman. I really don't know what prompted me do this, but I knew this woman was relevant to something, somehow. I wrote, "I had a dream that was extremely real again, just like the ones I had in the old apartment. There was a woman with shoulder-length, highlighted hair. Her demeanor was cold and distant. Who is she, and why am I dreaming about her?" After writing it down, I let it go. I put the book in a drawer next to my bed. I had decided to keep a dream journal after having such nightmares in the old apartment. I felt it would greatly benefit me to look back on dreams and experiences.

It was now October 1. I was enjoying my new apartment, and life was going well for Hannah and me. I had made some new friends, and I continued to visit with Hank at the coffee shop every so often. The haunted apartment seemed like a distant and horrible nightmare. Though I tried to forget the experience and move on, I couldn't quite shake the fact that I had experienced something paranormal.

Up until then, I had kept my mouth shut, avoiding talking about my experiences with anyone other than Jenny. I had done what the apartment management company had asked me to do in exchange for a new living space. Kelly had moved to a different city, and I hadn't talked to her for a while.

I thought the ordeal was behind me, but I was mistaken.

Periodically, I would dream about the couple who appeared in my first dream, and the girl they tortured. I kept records of the dates and times in a dream journal. I continued to be frightened when I thought about what I had witnessed during the nightmares. I couldn't imagine why I continued to have these nightmares. In my soul, I knew the dreams held some significance, but I wasn't sure what to make of them just yet.

I went to the coffee shop to visit with the old boys sometime in mid-October. Hank was there, sitting at his usual table.

"How are you today, Hank?" I asked. Hank said he was happy to see me.

"Seeing a cute little girl today was just what I needed to perk me up," he told me. He invited us to join him for a cup of tea. We sat down in the circle of old-timers, drinking our tea and listening to their everyday chatter and political debate. Hank sat drinking his coffee slowly that morning. I could tell his spirits were really low, and that something was on his mind.

"How is your wife today?" I asked.

"Not too good," he replied. I asked him if he wanted to tell me any old-time stories about Chico. He said, "I don't quite feel up to it, honey. Why don't you tell me something about you?"

"Can I tell you a story about my grandmother?"

"That sounds like a good conversation. Tell me about her, honey," he said.

"My grandmother was a wonderful, fun, loving woman. She was accepting of everyone, no matter what their circumstances. She would give you the shirt off her back if you needed it. I sure miss her."

"So your grandmother passed?" he asked.

"Yes, she did, in 1997. I was with her. I actually held her hand as she made the transition to heaven. I don't want to offend you, but there is more to the story, if you want to hear it."

I could tell by the look on Hank's face that my story had taken him out of his own misery for a minute.

He smiled at me and said, "I would love to hear more."

I continued. "I am certain there is something greater than me out there. I call it God; some people call it their higher power. I am confident there is an afterlife of some kind, though I don't really understand it."

Hank listened intently as I told him the story of Hannah's birth, and how my grandmother had come to me in a dream to announce her arrival.

My story prompted Hank to open up about his own life. He started talking about his loving wife and the long life he had shared with her.

"I am certain there is an afterlife as well," he said. "As a child, I had a visit from my grandmother after her death. She came to me while I was crying, sitting next to the creek.

"Grandma said, 'Hank boy, I am on the other side now, but I am still with you. I will give you signs, so you will know I haven't gone far.'"

Hank continued, "Throughout my life, I have encountered signs that convinced me she was, like she said, not too far away. And because of that, I am certain that when my loving wife passes on, she will come to me and let me know that everything is okay. We have a special sign only the two of us know about. When I receive it, I will know she is safe with God."

I felt a real sense of peace as Hank spoke with a commanding voice, certain in what he believed. As I sat there pondering what Hank had just said, I wondered if other people who had passed on could give us signs.

Hank then said, "I believe that if we live our lives doing good to ourselves and others, good will come; if we live a deceptive and cunning life, evil will come back to us."

I thought to myself, *How simple a concept. Is it really that easy? Is Hank talking about karma?* Somehow, Hank's simple, insightful, spiritual concept brought to mind the nightmares I had experienced along with the story Fred had shared with Kelly and me about the couple from Red Bluff.

I thought, *signs*. Both our grandmothers gave us signs and in that moment the haunted incident at my former apartment popped into my mind; I wasn't quite ready to blurt out, "*I lived in a haunted house, what do you think about that!?*" So instead I said, "Hank, I understand that you've lived in Chico for your whole life. Do you remember a story about a couple who abducted a young woman and held her as a sex slave? I lived where she used to live and one of the longtime residents shared a little bit with me, however he couldn't quite remember all the details."

"Yes, I am very familiar with the story," Hank said. "It made local and national news."

My stomach sank as Hank told me a story similar to the one Fred had shared with me.

"Yeah, a couple from Red Bluff captured a young woman back in the seventies and held her as a sex slave for seven years. I recall they had made a coffin, and she lived in it under their bed. I believe there was another young woman living in Chico who went missing and was never found or heard from again. The couple was supposedly connected to her disappearance as well. Why are you interested in this twisted old story?"

I prefaced my response with, "Hank, now I don't want you to think I am nuts."

"Honey, we are all a little nuts, or we wouldn't be here living on this magnificent planet, now would we?" he kindly responded with a giggle.

Hank's understanding nature made it easy to share my story; however, I was convinced that once the group of men sitting with us at the table heard me say "haunted," they were going to laugh me out of the coffee shop and drive me to the nearest loony bin.

I mustered the courage to say, "Well, Hank, I lived in an apartment on the north side of town. When I moved into the apartment, I started to have terrorizing nightmares of torture and abduction. At first I thought I might be losing my mind," I said with a nervous laugh, "I tried to basically tell myself it was stress, but then suddenly it became more. It actually escalated into strange paranormal activity, and here is the kicker, Hank. I wasn't the only one who experienced these anomalies."

Hank and the others looked at me for a few minutes. One of the older men laughed and said, "Sounds like you young people might have had quite a party. What kind of drugs were you and your friends on?" Hank looked at his friend and said, "Shut your old mouth Max, let the girl tell her story."

My voice cracked as I continued, "Hank, you said you believed in an afterlife. Do you think my experience could hold a deeper meaning…a sign?"

Hank looked at me with a smile on his face and conviction in his eyes. "Honey, I know there are deeper meanings and signs. You are not crazy—you might be on to something. Keep track of your dreams, and write down all your experiences!"

The men at the table stared at us. Max said, "Hank, do you really believe in this kind of nonsense?"

"I am banking on it," he replied with a strange little smile. I knew he was thinking about his wife. "This young lady isn't nuts—she had a real life-changing experience! She is here at our table for a reason! I believe that spirits sometimes contact us after passing. Maybe a person who passed has unfinished business, or maybe God just wants to remind us that there is a heaven awaiting us."

I sat there in the moment, listening to Hank, thinking I was sure lucky to be in the presence of a wise man, a man similar to my grandfather. Hank then said, "Jodi, you were given dreams, visions, and an experience that not many people have, or if they do, they are afraid to share it, for fear someone will think they are crazy. I believe God and your guardian angels want you to help solve a long-forgotten mystery—a mystery that has hurt many lives and people over the years. Don't be afraid. Trust, and be guided by a higher power.

"Maybe you should explore your dreams and start to research. From what I remember, there are many mysteries surrounding the crime that occurred in Red Bluff. If I were you, I would start to research the local newspapers."

After Hank's insightful speech, I felt relieved and cried a little.

"Hank," I said, "thank you for sharing your beliefs with me. You give me hope that I am not alone in what I have experienced, or in what I believe."

I think our conversation not only gave me hope, but it gave Hank renewed hope in an afterlife, too.

After the conversation with Hank, Hannah started getting restless. We had been there for a couple of hours, and that was long enough for a small child. I bid the good ol' boys goodbye and said that it was time I headed home for the day.

"I hope to see you soon; I can't wait to hear more stories," Hank said.

When I got home, I laid Hannah down for a nap. Then, as Hank had suggested, I called the local newspaper, the *Enterprise-Record*. A nice girl who worked in the editorial department answered. I asked her if she was familiar with an old case from the seventies involving a couple from Red Bluff who had kept a sexual slave. The staffer was young, just out of college, and wasn't aware of any stories like that, but she promised to do some research to see what she could come up with.

The next phone call was to another local newspaper: the *Chico News and Review*. The man who answered the phone told me he knew a little about the story of the sex slave, and how a possibly related story was one of ten unsolved murder cases in Butte County. My heart started pounding, and my throat went dry when I heard the word "murder."

"What do you mean, 'murder'?" I asked. "I thought it was a sex crime?"

"Yeah, we did a story a few years back on a missing girl connected to the couple, who was presumed to be dead." I had known a girl had possibly gone missing, but this was the first time I heard the words *murder* or *dead!* I think this is when reality sank in.

My mouth was so dry, I could hardly talk. I said, "Please, sir, I need to know more. When did this happen?"

"Sometime in the early eighties. All I can remember is that it happened in Red Bluff and was connected somehow to Chico."

The paper didn't keep records from that far back in their office, so he suggested I go to the Chico State Library, which kept old copies of the paper.

"Good luck," he said. "I hope you find what you're looking for."

When I hung up the phone, my heart started racing. I started to have a panic attack. *Could it be true? Is what he said true? Is there a missing girl presumed dead?* My heart raced as I tried to swallow. I couldn't put the pieces together. I wondered how the people in Red Bluff were involved.

I sat nervously on the floor in my apartment, wondering how I had gotten involved in such a weird story. I wondered what I could do. I was just a mom—what was I supposed to do?

I sat on my living room floor for a couple of hours, thinking about what Hank and Fred had told me about this situation. I thought about my paranormal experiences and dreams. Could there be more to this experience that I needed to explore? I thought back to what Hank had told me earlier about signs from the afterlife, and how the missing parts of a mystery long forgotten might still be waiting to be discovered. I prayed: *God, I don't know how this is supposed to unfold, but I am here to assist to the best of my abilities. Guide me. Show me what to do.*

It was Halloween. I noticed kids dressed up in costumes roaming the apartment complex getting ready for a day of trick-or-treat. Pumpkins lit up my windows and decorations adorned my front door. I was readying for the little ghouls, goblins, witches, and fairies to soon ring my doorbell. Thoughts regarding the world of unknown and unexplained lurked in my mind, when suddenly the phone rang.

"Hello, Miss Foster, this is Carol, from the Chico *Enterprise-Record*. I spoke with you earlier in the month. After our conversation, I did some research, and I came up with some fascinating information that might be of interest to you. Do you have a minute?"

Right then I heard a knock at my door. I was caught off guard by the phone call and simultaneous knock, I said, "Hi Carol, wow, yes, hum...darn it, could you hold on for a minute, I have some kids at my door needing candy." My heart was racing in anticipation of the call, but I had to attend to the costumed spooks. I rushed to the door. "Trick or treat!" they exclaimed. I grabbed the bowl of candy and let them have at it. "Happy Halloween. Starting a little early, huh? My, don't you look scary," I exclaimed, then shut the door, and rushed back to the phone. "Sorry to keep you waiting Carol."

"That's okay; it's that time of year. Well I wanted to let you know that the information I found is regarding a couple who had captured and held captive a woman by the name of Colleen Stan. Apparently the couple had kept her in a homemade coffin underneath their bed and had forced her to serve as a sex slave for seven years in Red Bluff. The couple's names were Janice and Cameron Hooker. Cameron Hooker is in prison, serving 104 years for the abduction and kidnapping of Colleen, however, the wife wasn't convicted of any crime, because she had turned state's evidence and had been granted immunity."

I couldn't believe my ears. "Let me get this straight, I understand that the man is in prison, but the wife was set free due to her testimony against her husband?"

I was shaking; I felt a panic attack coming on. My lips were numb. I felt as if I were going to pass out as I spoke. I was trying to make sense in my mind of such horror, and how it correlated with my old apartment. I calmly asked, "By any chance was the couple connected in any way to my apartment complex?"

"Now, here's the mystery," she replied. "As it turns out, Cameron and Janice Hooker were also connected to a missing girl from Chico who went by the name of Madeline Isabella Johnson. They supposedly planned out the abduction and kidnapping of this poor girl. She was nineteen years old and from Ohio. She'd recently moved to Chico with her boyfriend to attend school at Chico State. She went missing on January 31, 1976, after leaving a flea market. Madeline had gotten into a fight with her boyfriend at the flea market and had decided to walk home. She lived in the exact apartment you did."

When the woman mentioned my old address, my knees buckled underneath me, and I fell to the kitchen floor, shaking.

I could hear the woman on the phone asking, "Are you there? Are you there?"

I was in a full-blown panic attack. Somehow, I grabbed the phone and said, "I am here. Please forgive me; this news just came as a shock to me. I wasn't expecting to hear this kind of information today."

The girl then said, "Here's another portion of the story for you to try to swallow: Johnson was presumed dead. However, her remains haven't been found to this day. Neither Cameron nor Janice Hooker have been convicted of her murder. However, Janice Hooker admitted to helping her husband abduct this young woman and bury her body."

"She was captured and murdered? Where did they take her? Where did they bury her?" I replied, trying to maintain my composure.

"The answers to your questions elude the police to this day. Janice supposedly took them to the location of her remains back in the eighties. In fact, she took them all over Chico on a wild-goose chase. Though Janice took them to different locations, she maintained that her memories were unclear due to stress and time."

"So you're saying this is still a cold case?"

"Yes, it remains an open cold case, twenty-four years later."

What I heard sounded surreal and unbelievable. Neither Janice nor Cameron Hooker had been convicted of murder because the police had never found a body? *Of course Janice didn't find the body. If she had, they would both be convicted of murder.*

"Before we hang up," the woman said, "I wanted to let you know that a book was written about the capture and abduction of Colleen Stan, their second victim. You might find a copy at the library—it's called *The Perfect Victim*. I hope this information is of help to you, Miss Foster."

I sat on the floor, leaning against the refrigerator, sweating, my heart and mind racing. Trying to digest all the information felt as though a knife had been stuck in my belly.

I thought about the numerous nightmares and supernatural encounters I had witnessed at my former apartment. Then I thought about something Hannah had said about an angel in the apartment. My body trembled, as I realized during that moment, without a shadow of doubt, that my child had seen a ghost, and she called her My Belle.

SIXTEEN

Halloween 2000

I sat at the City Plaza, a park in the middle of downtown Chico. The weather was cool and the air nippy. Fall had definitely arrived. I looked up at the leaves on the old trees, and noticed the changing color, the smell of smoke from a nearby wood stove lingering in the air. Many adults and children bustled around in costumes, getting ready to fill trick-or-treat bags with goodies. While I wait at the old, wooden gazebo, I looked out at my daughter, dressed up in her pretty pink princess costume, and all the other kids playing, then thought, *Regardless of my earlier conversation with Carol, I am still thankful to live in such a unique and great town.* Unfortunately, my newfound information weighed heavy on my mind and chest.

"Where is Jenny?" I looked at my watch. It was almost 6:00 p.m. "She was supposed to be here by now." I looked up from my watch, "Oh, there she is, Hannah." Jenny was dressed in a long, black witch costume, and Phillip was dressed like a superhero.

"Jenny, you're not going to believe what I am about to tell you. It is a true story that will make you remember Halloween 2000 for years to come."

She looked at me. "Give me a minute Jodi. For God's sake, I just got here. What now?"

"I was given some really creepy information today; but it might just explain a few things about my old apartment. I got a call from a girl who works for the newspaper; she told me about a couple who lived in Red Bluff by the name of Cameron and Janice Hooker. They shared a sadomasochistic relationship. Unfortunately, their sick relationship wasn't enough, so the couple went hunting for a victim…a sex slave."

"Are you kidding me? Is this some kind of Halloween joke?" Jenny asked.

"The girl they captured and tried to enslave lived in my old apartment."

Jenny looked at me in disbelief. "Come on, are you serious? You're not joking?"

"No, Jenny! Now listen to me; this is a true story!" I exclaimed. "The couple also captured a woman named Colleen Stan, whom they kept in a coffin and used as a sex slave for seven years."

The look on Jenny's face was one of pure shock. She screamed at me, "Are you for real? Sex slaves?"

"Shhh... don't yell. Yes, sex slaves. I just spent the past few hours trying to digest the information myself!"

We both sat quietly staring at each other in a strange, suspended animation. Kids and people in costumes surrounded us. After a few minutes, a cold breeze started to blow and I was brought back to reality.

"Jenny, are you okay?"

"Yes, but how could a couple keep a sex slave under their bed, alive, for seven years? What happened to the girl who lived in your apartment?"

"The wife admitted to helping her husband kidnap, murder, and bury the girl. The authorities searched for her remains, but nothing came of their attempts."

"Oh my God. You've got to be kidding me, Jodi. Well, this explains a lot. No wonder so many strange things happened in there!"

We sat silent most of the night, deep in our own thoughts, both of us trying our best to give the kids a fun-filled night of Halloween excitement. I wanted to create happy childhood memories of downtown Chico for our kids, even if I had started my Halloween by learning about sex slaves and a dead young woman.

Jenny turned to me and said, "I have an idea. When I get home, I will call my cousin again and tell him about the missing girl and what we found out. He will know what to do. He will probably give us another ritual to help bring her soul peace. Tomorrow, November 1, is when many cultures celebrate the spirits of ancestors and saints who have passed over. It seems fitting to honor her spirit then. I am sure we will have to go to the apartment to do the ritual."

"Are you nuts? I don't want to go over there!"

After moving out, I really didn't want to have anything to do with the old place again.

But Jenny made a reasonable argument. "I know a prayer and cleansing would have more of an effect if we were in the environment."

Though I was frightened, a part of me knew she was right. *Maybe if we acknowledged her soul on this sacred day, known as the Day of the Dead, her restless spirit would be able to move on, and finally rest in peace.*

"Hey Jenny, did it occur to you that the apartment might be occupied…and I don't mean by a ghost, but an actual human?"

"Oh crap, I didn't think of that." She paused a moment. Okay Jodi, tomorrow call the complex and ask if it is vacant. If it is, ask if we could take a look at it. We'll pose as possible renters."

"Really, Jenny? That's your plan?"

The following day, Jenny called her cousin, and I reluctantly called the apartment complex, which was now under new management. I asked if there was a vacant downstairs apartment for rent, that was not close to the street. I can't say that I was surprised to find out that the exact apartment unit that I had lived in a mere few months earlier was indeed vacant.

So I asked if my friend and I could go over to the apartment later that afternoon to take a look inside. Our plan was now set in motion.

On the afternoon on November 1st, we drove to the apartment complex to perform a ritual given to Jenny by her cousin from Cuba. As we drove, I could feel my heart pounding—as if it were going to jump out of my chest. Even though I was panicking, my motivation was to help Madeline pass on to God. I kept telling myself that the paranormal activity was only a sign; it wasn't a scary spirit. It was the spirit of a young woman whose life had been cut short. She was trying to get my attention, and all those anomalies had been clues. I just hadn't gotten it at the time, because I couldn't make sense of it within my fundamentalist Christian mind-set.

My fear of the unknown had scared me while I lived in the apartment. I was still scared of the unknown, but now I had a little knowledge to pacify the anxiety. I knew the missing girl had a name, and I had my best friend with me.

Posing as renters, we were now at the front door of my old apartment. Armed with white candles and flowers, a prayer we had written, anointing oil, salt, and a small hand drum, we opened the door to the old place. My heart was racing. I was frightened and strangely excited. I wasn't sure if the spirit of the missing girl was going to be waiting. Part of me was thinking, maybe even hoping, she was going to open the door and say, "*Hello, ladies. I was waiting for your arrival.*"

Jenny and I held hands and walked into the old vacant apartment together, quickly shutting the door behind us before someone caught wind of what we were doing. I felt her hand sweating and her body shaking as we made our way to the living room to perform our ritual. We stood there together, holding hands. I took in a few deep breaths, remembering how I had felt the last time I was here. I let out a sigh of relief. Jenny did, too.

Jenny turned to me and said, "Let's do this thing. My cousin said to make a salt circle around us, and then light the candles, then we are to set the vase with flowers along with the drum in the center next to us. We are to kneel down, and then start to pray."

Jenny hit the drum then said, "We are here to honor your spirit."

"Jodi, you pray in English. I will pray in Spanish."

We read the prayer out loud together.

"Dear God, here we are together with the Holy Spirit, asking for the spirit of Madeline Isabella Johnson to find her way to you. She needs rest now. We are asking for her safe return home to you. Please allow her spirit the opportunity to pass on, knowing you are a loving God who opens your arms to her beautiful soul. *She is loved and wanted by you.*"

I said, "Madeline, you have been wronged in this life-time. Jenny and I are aware of you, and we know you are missing. I am so sorry for what happened to you."

Jenny beat on the drum and then said, "Madeline, go toward the light. A tunnel will appear; walk through. You will find family, friends, and guardian angels waiting for you."

After our prayer, I felt a warm, calm breeze pass over our heads. I didn't feel scared now. I did, however, feel a deep sadness, as though a good friend had said goodbye. We sat in the salt circle together in the old apartment, weeping. The energy was light and serene. Jenny and I both thought that we must have helped this poor girl pass over.

As soon as we were finished, we quickly got up from the salt circle and walked out the front door, holding hands and laughing. A sense of accomplishment washed over me. It was as though the burdens of the past few months were gone. I believed Madeline Isabella Johnson had been able to move on, thanks to our acknowledgment and prayer. As I walked to the car, I was under the impression that the apartment was no longer haunted and our job was over. I believed in my heart that I would never have to experience the dreams or worries associated with that apartment ever again.

I was wrong.

Little did I know that over the next few years, Madeline's story and my paranormal experience would touch so many lives. I would soon encounter more visions, dreams, intrigue, and many other people connected to the fascinating mystery. Living in a haunted house had changed my life. I continued to question my experience, religion, and my understanding of God.

I continued to visit my buddies at the coffee shop. One day, Hank said, "Jodi, I know you're looking for a job; you might want to apply here. I know the owner and I could put in a good word." I applied and got the job, thanks in part to my newfound buddies.

I worked at the coffee shop and continued to visit with my friends. I talked to Jenny and Jessica almost every day. Although sharing the alarming incidents in the old apartment was a strong common bond, we were all moving forward in our lives to new experiences.

I had met a nice man named Ted. He was in his forties, with wild, curly, graying hair that came to his shoulders. He was tall, with crystal blue eyes, and a gap between his teeth. His was an intellectual, well read and educated. He taught yoga and reminded me of a college professor. I had met him a few months earlier through some friends. He would come to visit me while I worked. We started dating, and before long we found out I was expecting a child. Ted had two other kids, Lucas, eight, and Jonah, six. I had Hannah. I was extremely excited to find out about the pregnancy. Ted was excited, too. He had thought he was finished having babies, but the universe and the spirit of our child had other ideas. Soon we were a blended family of five with one on the way. Life was good.

One day, while taking a nap, I had a dream. A baby boy came to me, smiling and happy. He told me that his name was Sam. When I awoke from the dream, Ted was lying next to me. Excited, he said, "I was waiting for you to wake up. I want to tell you about a vision I had today while riding my bike. I know we are going to have a baby boy, and his name starts with an S."

I started to laugh and said, "Yes, Ted, I know. I had a dream just now, and our baby's name is Sam!" He joined me in my laughter.

On June 5, 2001, Ted and I delivered a smiling baby boy, whom we named Sam.

Sam, and the visions that preceded his birth, got me thinking again. *Why are some paranormal events such blessings while others are so frightening? Is it only a matter of perception?* Looking into the eyes of my new baby boy, I felt blessed. I had him to cuddle and hold in my arms. Somehow in that blessed moment, holding Sam, I realized that Madeline Johnson had been someone's daughter and baby once. At that moment of realization, I knew that my journey with Madeline wasn't over; it had only been put on hold.

I wanted to tell someone about my dreams and about what I had experienced. *But who is going to take me seriously? Who would believe me?*

Ted suggested that I find the book written about the sex slave, called *The Perfect Victim*. I thought that maybe someday I would, but right then, I wanted to focus on being a new mom.

SEVENTEEN

Revealing Photos

Throughout the next few years, many of the friends I had made came and went. After falling ill, Fred moved away to live with his kids. I would see Hank off and on after his wife died. He would tell me about the signs his wife had sent him from the afterlife. Kelly and I never really kept in touch after our experience at the old apartment.

I encountered people I trusted, with whom I would share my crazy paranormal adventure. I would explain that I had not been the only one who had encountered paranormal activity while living in the old apartment. Others who had lived there before me have recalled similar experiences. Most people knew the story about Colleen Stan, who had been a captive in a box for seven years, but no one remembered Madeline Isabella Johnson or knew that her remains had never been recovered. When I shared the story, most everyone was shocked, especially when I shared how Cameron and Janice Hooker had never been convicted of Johnson's murder. That part of the story remained a mystery.

One day, when Ted was out thrift-store shopping, he happened to come across a copy of *The Perfect Victim*. The story was written by the prosecuting attorney, Christine Maguire, regarding the trial and abduction of Colleen Stan.

Ted rushed home and said, "Open your hand." I did, and he handed me the book. I looked down and read the cover. My stomach sank. Up until now, I had never seen the book or any pictures of Cameron or Janice Hooker. This was way before everything was put on the internet.

Ted said, "Before we crack open the book, you should get out your dream journal, so we can see how your nightmares correlate to events in the book."

Over the years, I had continued to keep a record of these dreams. I ran to the back bedroom and grabbed my dream journal. Ted and I sat together on the living room floor after the kids were asleep, ready to look through the book. I was unbelievably panicked. I wanted to look at the pictures, but I was afraid.

I asked Ted, "Do you think you could look first? I am too freaked out."

I started to cry as I heard him crack the book open. I closed my eyes. Ted turned to the center of the book, where the picture section was.

"It's okay, Jodi. Your experience is behind you. Let's look forward to a new understanding."

"I want to, Ted, but it's hard. I want to understand—I do. I really do. I want to be okay with everything that happened at the haunted apartment. But I also feel like a little kid who wants to run and hide."

When I finally had enough courage to look, the first photo I saw was that of Cameron Hooker. I immediately recognized him from my nightmares. My heart started to race and my throat started to tighten, just like in my nightmares. He was creepy—he looked like a serial killer or child molester.

Ted reached over and hugged me. "You're okay. Let's keep going."

He turned the page to reveal another picture; it was of a light-haired woman with round glasses, dowdy clothing, and a distant gaze in her eyes. The caption read, "Janice Hooker."

I was shaking as I looked at Ted and cried, "This is them! This is them! It's the couple from my nightmares!"

Having a book in front of me with the pictures of Janice and Cameron Hooker made my dreams and experiences seem all too real again. There were pictures of the torture chamber, of a head box, of whips and chains, and also of Colleen Stan. There was no photo of Madeline Isabella Johnson. It was painful to see the faces of the couple who had kept and killed a sex slave. I couldn't fathom how anyone could do such horrific acts. Looking at that book was too much for me.

"Ted, do you think that you could read the book for me? I don't think I can do it."

"Okay, honey. I will go to the coffee shop."

Ted went to the coffee shop to read the book. After he finished, he told me that the text had been excruciating to read because it talked in detail about the torture and pain that Colleen Stan had endured. Ted had read how Janice, after seven years, had turned her husband in to the Red Bluff police for the kidnapping of Colleen Stan. Janice had gone along with her husband in abducting Colleen and holding her captive. Janice had used her as a babysitter, house slave, sex partner, and source of income. She had even insisted that Colleen call her ma'am. But even after all of Colleen's fearful, yet dedicated years, Janice remained jealous of the sexual attention Cameron gave to Colleen. Janice was now fearful that she might lose Cameron because he was considering having a child with Colleen.

Ted told me that Janice had gone to a pastor at a church she had attended. She had revealed to him the sick and twisted truth about her relationship with Cameron and the crimes they had committed together.

And during the trial and conviction of Cameron Hooker, Madeline Isabella Johnson's name was revealed. Janice asked for immunity regarding her involvement with Colleen's kidnapping. However, it wasn't clear if Janice was granted immunity regarding her involvement in the alleged murder of Madeline. The book confirmed that Madeline had indeed lived in the same apartment complex as I had. She had lived there with her boyfriend in January 1976.

Janice, although granted immunity regarding the Colleen Stan case, wasn't able to provide the police with the whereabouts of Madeline's remains. Other than Janice Hooker's story, the police had no evidence regarding Madeline's abduction, murder, and burial. It was though Madeline had never existed. And because the prosecution had Hooker for Colleen's abduction, it was as if what happened to Madeline was forgotten.

Ted's account of the book worried me. My paranormal experience was now even more real. After comparing my dreams with details in *The Perfect Victim*, I asked, "What do you think, Ted? Should I go to the authorities with my experiences and nightmares?"

Ted didn't think the time was right. "Continue to keep up on your journal, and talk to me and your girlfriends about it. When the time is right to take it to the authorities, you will know."

I had mixed emotions about *The Perfect Victim*, but I knew it was another piece to a puzzle that continued to remain a mystery in my life.

EIGHTEEN

It's Time for Counseling

My experiences with the paranormal had, at times, made me question my sanity. Ted and I were having struggles in our relationship and had recently separated. We were doing our best to co-parent, but at this point I felt I needed professional advice. Fortunately, I was lucky enough to find a counselor who was able and willing to see me. I was finally ready to open up, and I had much to discuss: my haunted apartment, an alcoholic mother, my dreams and nightmares, and my off-and-on struggle with panic attacks and agoraphobia. At times I wondered if I was insane…or perhaps that just maybe I actually had some kind of God-given gift, whatever the case may be, I was ready, able, and willing to explore my truth.

I remember having a lump in the back of my throat the day I walked in to the counseling office to tell my story. The counselor's office was decorated sparsely, with small, dark, wooden tables and minimal decor. The walls were painted a lovely shade of green. The room had a Zen Buddhist feel to it.

Her name was Stephanie. Right away, she let me know I was in a safe environment and that I would be able to talk to her about anything I needed to. "Nice to meet you Jodi, come on in and have a seat."

"I don't really know where to begin. I have so many things I want to talk about."

"Just take your time. Let's get to know each other. This is a process. We are not in any hurry," Stephanie said.

I let out a sigh of relief and just sat and cried for a few minutes.

Finally, I gathered my courage, took in a deep breath, and said, "I am a little confused; that is why I am here. I grew up as a fundamentalist Christian, and I experienced something that makes me question reality. Do you believe in the paranormal? Do you believe in ghosts or haunted houses? Have you ever counseled anyone regarding such paranormal experiences or been to a place you thought might be haunted?"

To my surprise, her response was, "Yes, I have encountered people who have claimed to have had paranormal experiences. In fact, some people, called parapsychologists, study the paranormal."

"Are people who see ghosts insane?"

"There are some people who are not in touch with reality," she said. "However, there are situations that are not explainable, and in those cases, paranormal investigation might be of benefit. I actually counseled a man who'd had some strange experiences. I felt he might benefit from a professional nurse and clairvoyant I had occasionally worked with."

"What is a clairvoyant?" I asked.

"A clairvoyant is someone who can see or sense things beyond the five senses. The best analogy would be how a dog or cat can sense things. Some humans also possess these qualities."

I knew I was in the right place for my mental-health needs.

In time, after establishing trust, I was able to share my experiences with my counselor. I was able to understand those strange occurrences and know I wasn't insane. In fact, I actually had a God-given talent! I was a sensitive and loving soul with some psychic abilities. In addition, I realized that it wasn't my responsibility to understand everything—I only needed to do my best and learn and understand to the best of my abilities.

From 2002 until 2006, I continued to go to counseling. I read many books on different religions and psychic abilities. I was a spiritual student and mom of four kids now. My experience in the old apartment continued to fuel my desire to learn more about the spiritual life. Madeline Johnson influenced my spiritual growth.

One day, Ted, who had been contemplating my paranormal dilemma, decided to give me one of his treasured yoga books, which he thought I might find inspirational. It was called *I Am That*, by Swami Muktananda. The book inspired me and helped me to see life in a new way. After reading it, I wondered how much my fears, due to my fundamentalist Christian upbringing, had influenced my experience at the apartment in Chico. From that moment forward, Ted encouraged me to search out and help Madeline Isabella Johnson. From what I understood, her remains were still missing, and she had been forgotten. I wanted to bring her story to light; I wanted her to finally rest in peace and have a voice.

On October 27, 2007, I was visiting with my girlfriend Lucy. She and I were sitting on my front porch talking about the weather and watching my kids play in the front yard. Lucy had been out of town for a few years, working and caring for her ailing father, so I hadn't seen her in a while. Lucy had a great sense of humor and could always make me laugh. I was surprised to find out she had recently moved back and was living just around the corner from me. It was nice to visit and to rekindle our friendship.

The air was crisp, and leaves started to change color. Fall was in the air. It was almost Halloween again. Lucy and I sat, talking about Halloween and what, if anything, it meant to each of us.

"One of my fondest Halloween memories is of almost delivering Hannah at midnight," I said. "Yeah, autumn is my favorite time of year. It brings me a sense of well-being after a long, hot Chico summer."

"The only bad experience I ever had during this time of year," I continued, "was during Halloween 2000. I received information about Janice and Cameron Hooker and their involvement with Colleen Stan and the alleged murder of Madeline Isabella Johnson. I told you about my paranormal experience and the connection to my old apartment, didn't I?"

"No," Lucy said. "I don't think you did."

For the next couple of hours, Lucy and I sat on my front porch. I recounted the horrible experience.

"How creepy to receive such strange information on Halloween," she said.

"I just about had a heart attack. You know, I wondered over the years if Halloween were significant to Madeline or if it had any relevance to the unsolved case."

"I know one way to find out," Lucy said. "Let's get on my computer. Surely, after all these years, there must be something online."

At this point in my spiritual studies and counseling, I was up for the challenge, although I still couldn't navigate a computer.

After a little internet surfing at Lucy's, we found the location of Cameron Hooker. He was in Corcoran State Prison, serving 104 years for the abduction and kidnapping of Colleen Stan. He had recently gone in front of the parole board, trying to get out on good behavior. We found out, thank God, that his parole was denied, although we read in a blog that due to prison overcrowding, it might only be a matter of time before he was out on the streets.

This knowledge sickened me and motivated my desire to research further. There seemed to be a lot of information about Colleen Stan, but only one paragraph about the Hookers' involvement with Madeline Isabella Johnson. There were no pictures or blog posts regarding Madeline Isabella. It was as though she didn't exist. Why was that? After doing more Net browsing, Lucy found out that Janice, who had confessed to kidnapping Colleen Stan and also helping abduct and murder Madeline Isabella Johnson, was a free woman.

"Lucy, this is horrible," I said. "It still bothers me that Janice, who admitted helping with these crimes, can roam free? This is so unfair. I know she turned state's evidence against Cameron, but come on! How does she not serve any time for her involvement?"

"That's a good question," Lucy said. "It says here that she claimed to have something called Stockholm syndrome. But that doesn't really make sense, especially if you know what Stockholm syndrome is."

"What is it?" I replied.

"The name is from a 1973 hostage incident in Stockholm, Sweden. At the end of six days of captivity in a bank, several kidnap victims actually resisted rescue attempts and refused to testify against their captor. Captives begin to identify with their captors as a defense mechanism, due to fear of violence."

"Well, that makes sense if we are talking about Colleen, but I don't see how that defense applies to Janice or how that could get her off for murder."

"Yeah, it doesn't make sense to me, either."

"Oh, my God, Lucy, I just thought of something. I wonder where Janice is today."

Up until then, I had never thought about the Hookers' whereabouts. But in Lucy, I now had a friend who was equally interested in researching the scenario.

It was getting late, so we made a plan to get together after Halloween to continue investigating.

The prospect of knowing more was exciting. I had been tortured by the mystery for years, and at one point in my life, having paranormal experiences and clairvoyant abilities had been scary. Now it was intriguing—an adventure full of possibilities.

———

Good old Jenny had continued to be a support to me. She and Lucy and I got together two days before Thanksgiving to discuss the story in its entirety. I recall sitting at my kitchen table, which was decorated with autumn leaves and white candles, while sipping tea, eating cookies, and laughing with the girls.

"I think I should bring out my dream journal," I said.

"That's an excellent idea. Go get it," Jenny said.

Together we sat, reading over memories and dreams from years before of the nightmares and experiences at the apartment. I had written about Cameron Hooker's perversions and his callous disregard for life. He seemed like evil personified. I had described Janice Hooker's distant, glazed look. I had noted the times and dates of the paranormal events and horrid nightmares.

Lucy had brought her laptop computer and was looking at a web page about the Hookers. Next to Lucy, Jenny and I continued to flip through my dream journal. All of a sudden, I realized one strange detail that made me take a second glance at both my journal and the web page Lucy was looking at. The date of a certain paranormal event in the journal matched that displayed on Lucy's computer screen. The jarring date: February 1.

I had moved into the downstairs apartment on February 1. That same night, I had my first paranormal occurrence. According to the story on the computer, the Hookers gave Madeline Isabella Johnson a ride on January 31, 1976. Shivers ran down my spine as I read over the account of her disappearance and looked at the dates in my journal. *How could a paranormal event occur with such synchronicity twenty-four years after the original event?*

"Girls, look here," I said. "I found a strange coincidence. I moved into the apartment exactly twenty-four years to the day after Madeline Isabella Johnson went missing."

Lucy replied, "Jodi, there's something here about Madeline possibly being murdered sometime between January 31 and February 2."

"Oh, my God, Jodi, that's no coincidence," Jenny said.

We continued to pore over the journal and the computer that evening. I felt as if we were a team of crazed girl detectives huddled together in my living room. None of us had a clue about what we might uncover, but the thrill of the chase was enough to fuel our desire for another meeting.

It was getting late, so we planned another get-together for after Thanksgiving. I invited Lucy to spend Thanksgiving Day with me and my family, since she was going to be alone.

The holiday was a nice, relaxing day filled with family and friends. That weekend, after Thanksgiving, Lucy had a friend come into town from the Bay Area. She and the friend were going out on the town and invited me to go with them. The three of us went out for dinner and dancing. We had a great time. When we all parted ways at the evening's end, I decided the weather was nice enough to walk home.

Walking home, the air was crisp. Winter was just around the corner. Many houses were decorated for the coming Christmas holiday. While I walked, I reminisced about my life and how lucky I felt to have such a great family and kind friends. Chico still felt like home.

That night, I awoke suddenly to the smoke alarm going off.

Hannah and Sam came out of their bedrooms and said, "Mom, is there a fire?"

The kids opened the front door and sat on the front porch as I searched the house for smoke or a fire. I replied, "Everything looks fine, kids. It's cold out there; come back in. I checked the entire house and the batteries in the alarm. Everything checks out."

I got the kids back in bed and then headed to bed myself. As soon as I lay my head on the pillow, the alarm went off again. When I sat up, I looked to my right. There, sitting on my nightstand, was my cell phone. A blue light was flashing to notify me that I had a voice message. When I picked up the phone to check the message, the smoke detector stopped beeping. I knew something was wrong, so I checked the voicemail immediately. It was an older woman—Lucy's mother. She was crying and asking for help in contacting her daughter. She said it was an emergency but didn't go into details. I told Hannah that I needed to go get Lucy.

I remember running up the stairs to her second-story apartment at about 4:00 a.m., yelling "Lucy, your mom called my cell phone. There's been an emergency." She immediately opened the door.

"Oh, my God, Jodi, what's wrong?" she cried.

Lucy opened her door. We sat down on the floor together, and I dialed her mother, who lived in Las Vegas. She had tragic news: Lucy's father had died of a heart attack a couple of hours earlier.

I held Lucy close as she spoke to her mother and cried. "Not Daddy…not my daddy! I just talked to him last night, Mama. He was fine!"

Her reaction reminded me of my grandfather's unexpected death. I tried to comfort her as she yelled and wailed in agony, "God, it's not fair. Why? Why?"

As Lucy continued to cry, I thought about how different types of deaths affected emotions. I had been more prepared for my grandmother's death than my grandfather's because I had known she was dying of cancer. The difference between an unexpected death and a death from long illness was enormous. Grams and I had been able to tell each other how much we loved and meant to each other. We were able to talk about the other side, and of being with God. I recalled Hank, from the coffee shop, mentioning the special time he had spent with his wife before—and signs after—her passing.

This got me thinking about different types of death and the energy that surrounds a passing. I had read about residual energy during some of my spiritual studies. Residual energy, also known as an imprint, is supposedly the product of an emotional incident or a violent event. Just as an iron remains hot long after it is turned off, strong energy seems to be stored in physical surroundings. *Could the energy surrounding Madeline Isabella Johnson's violent and emotional death be the reason for the haunting at the apartment complex?*

NINETEEN

Things Start to Make Sense

The holidays were over, and 2008 had arrived. I was looking forward to enjoying a nice, warm winter with the kids. My birthday was just around the corner—I was going to turn forty-one. I was talking with Hannah about birthday plans when she said, "Hey, Mom, I was thinking about how strange it is that your birthday coincides with the disappearance of Madeline Isabella Johnson. And another weird coincidence is that your grandfather died on the exact same day in January."

"Oh, my God, Hannah, you're right," I said. "For the life of me I don't know why I hadn't put that together before now—that is a really strange coincidence. I wonder if Madeline Johnson and I have some kind of connection because of the tragedies we both encountered on the same day in 1976."

"Don't you think that's kind of weird, Mom?" Hannah replied "Maybe they met in God's waiting room?"

I laughed, "Yeah it is kind of weird, kid. Hey, let's lie down by the heater; I am feeling a little tired. Go get your brother and a blanket."

We all lay by the heater together talking about birthdays and laughed about how old I was getting. After a while, the kids and I drifted off to sleep in front of the cozy heater, on top of our blanket.

That evening, I had a vivid dream. It was about an older Native American man. He met me in the cow pasture next to my childhood house in Berry Creek. I remember that I could see him from a distance. He was wearing buckskin pants and had a deer hide blanket wrapped around him. I could see five feathers braided into his long, black hair. He approached me and asked me to sit with him in the open field next to my old house. So I did.

He looked me straight in the eyes—it felt as if he were reaching deep into my soul. I knew this was his way of communicating with me. I wasn't frightened at all; this man was strangely familiar. I knew what he was saying even though he didn't speak out loud. He told me his name: Wind Warrior. He was an elder in his Maidu tribe. His people lived in the mountains of Berry Creek. His relatives and friends in neighboring tribes lived in Deer Creek and in the mountains of Shasta. These tribes migrated with the deer and hunted over many miles of mountains. He shared a story of how these people had been hunted by a certain important white man who had taken over their tribe's land. He had hunted the Native Americans, Wind Warrior explained, and kept the heads on the fences around his property as a warning sign.

"White people murdered my relatives. They ran us into caves in the mountains and killed us, young and old, like vermin." I didn't know why he was telling me this.

So I asked, "What does this have to do with me?"

"You will understand soon. I am one of your spirit guides.

"I have been with you since you were a small child. You ran away from me when you didn't understand. I was behind the old oak tree near the creek when you were walking to school with your sister. You were not ready to meet me until now. I continued to watch over and guide you through the years."

Wind Warrior told me something interesting during our meeting. It helped me understand my spirit on a deeper level. He shared with me insights about his land.

"The mountains have eyes. Certain land has magic and is used for ceremonies. A white girl was taken to our sacred land by an evil monster. He killed her and buried her small body in 1976. What this man didn't understand was that the mountains see and remember."

I continued to listen.

"Our spiritual ancestors were angered by what they saw: another selfish man taking life. The ancestors helped the young girl because she didn't understand what had happened to her."

"How did they help?" I asked respectfully.

"They showed her how to communicate in the spirit realm. She asked one of my grandfathers to help her get back home. She needed to contact her boyfriend. She had fought with him the last time they had been together. They were in love, and she wanted to tell him she was sorry."

"Someday you will understand how to use your energy to communicate spiritually. Grandfather showed her how to gather her energy, to affect electricity, and to also ring the phone. While the police were at Fred's house, questioning him, she tried to get his attention by way of phone."

"Why do I need to know this? Who is the girl?" I asked.

"The white girl's name is Madeline, but she had a special name that will be revealed to you in time. Your child has spoken this special name. Soon you will understand. You have been given a great gift that only now, as an adult, are you able to appreciate, because you have gone beyond your fear. Listen to the knowingness in the center of your being, that is where the Great Spirit resides. Also know that in the spiritual realm, there is no such thing as time…time is simply an illusion of the human experience."

Wind Warrior got up from the field where we had been sitting and walked off into tall pine trees. As soon as he disappeared, I immediately woke from my dream.

I was brought back to the reality of my living room, lying next to Sam and Hannah. It comforted me to know that Wind Warrior had been by my side since childhood as my spirit guide. The dream had been reminiscent of the encounter with my grandmother after her passing.

In the past seven years, I had come to terms with the fact that I had clairvoyant abilities. I had studied and read. I did meditation and got comfortable with the idea of being a sensitive person. I also realized, during that dream, that Hannah too had special God-given abilities.

I decided to say a prayer.

"God, I ask for divine guidance. I understand that I am not a perfect human being. I know that you have placed me in this situation for a reason. Please help me understand this vision I was given, because it doesn't fit into my fundamentalist Christian upbringing. Guide my steps as I move forward; I want to be able to share my clairvoyant abilities with those who need my help, but right now I am not sure how to do this. As a child I had these abilities but I suppressed them because I didn't understand them and I was scared. Now here I am, an adult, experiencing this same gift again. What do I do?"

After meeting Wind Warrior, I realized that God did not require me to be a perfect human in order to help him, nor did I have to understand the entirety of this vision. All I needed was to come from a place in my heart of truth and integrity, and that in time, God would take care of the rest.

TWENTY

The Face of a Ghost

I awoke to a surprise call from my friend Lucy on the morning of February 1. Apparently she had sent a note to a show called *Psychic Kids*. She had sent my phone number along with a brief story about me and Hannah.

The very next day I got a phone call from a woman named Linda who lived in New York and worked for the A&E network. She said she had received an interesting e-mail from a friend of mine telling her about my haunted apartment, and how as a child I had experienced paranormal activity. Lucy also indicated to Linda that Hannah, too, had some paranormal experiences and she might also have some psychic gifts.

Linda told me the network was doing a show on psychic kids and was interested in children who may have some psychic abilities. At this point, the word "psychic" bothered me. However, I saw this as an opportunity to learn more about clairvoyance. We talked about how my grandma came to visit before Hannah's birth, growing up in the mountains of Berry Creek next to a Native American cemetery, and my experiences with the spirit world. Then I told her the story of the haunted apartment where Hannah and I had lived in 2000 and described some of the extreme paranormal experiences.

"Jodi, this is a really fascinating story and I think it would make great TV. Let me talk with one of our executive producers. I would like to do some investigating."

We hung up and I waited. A couple of days went by and I was beginning to think that after their research, they concluded that we were a little too crazy to go on TV. I was wrong. Linda had done some research and found out that A&E had done a show called "Girl in the Box" about Colleen Stan.

I was shocked to hear that there had been a show dedicated to the story of Colleen Stan, detailing how she endured abduction, slavery, and torture. But they had nothing about Madeline—apparently this was where my kids and I came in. Linda said. "Our crew wants to come out and do a story on your haunted experiences. What do you think about that?"

"Well, I feel a bit uneasy about being on national television, and I'm a little worried that we might be portrayed as lunatics.

"I wanted to get Madeline's story out to the public, because she had been forgotten. And I hoped that by doing so, she may find peace. I hoped that others with similar experiences to mine might see the show, and find solace, knowing that there were others in the world who had experienced paranormal activity. Would it be okay if I thought about the offer for about a week?" Linda agreed. "Yes, take a week. But I need to know as soon as possible, so we can start making plans to come out to film."

A week later, I gave Linda a call to let her know I was interested in doing the documentary. A date was set for after Valentine's Day, and A&E was on its way.

After securing the plan for the show, I called Lucy to share the news. After Lucy, I called Jenny. During our conversation, Jenny said something poignant; "Jodi, do you remember Halloween 2000?"

"Ahhh, yeah, how could I ever forget it, that holiday will go down in mind as one of the weirdest ever. Why?"

"The girl from the *Enterprise-Record* told you that she had done some research on the Hooker criminal case, right? Well it occurred to me, that if she was able to find out information on the subject, that maybe we could too. Don't you think it's about time we went to the newspaper to do some research?"

The news of a Red Bluff kidnapping, torture, and sex-slavery story, dubbed "The Girl in the Box," grabbed national headlines during much of 1984, and continued to receive attention since, but Madeline Isabella Johnson was still forgotten.

"I agree. It's about time," I said. "And you know it might put things into perspective for me if I could finally see the face of the missing girl who haunted me for so many years. I wonder if there might be a picture of Madeline somewhere in the *Enterprise-Record's* archives. Her family must have filed a missing persons report with the police. And there was probably a picture somewhere."

"That's what I am thinking, Jodi. After we hang up, why don't you give them a call and see what you can find out?"

After Jenny hung up, I immediately called the *Enterprise-Record*. I was put in contact with a man named Doug Nelson. When Doug answered the phone, his voice was strong and commanding. I felt a little intimidated, but my need to research overruled my fright.

"Doug Nelson, how can I help you?" he said.

I cleared my throat and said, "Hello, Doug. My name is Jodi Foster. I am doing some research on a story from back in the eighties, regarding a woman by the name of Madeline Isabella Johnson and a couple by the name of Cameron and Janice Hooker."

"Are you the actress Jodie Foster?" he asked.

"No," I said with a laugh, "I am not the actress, but I am the real Jodi Foster. The actress's real name is Alicia." I replied with a giggle.

"Are you doing a paper for school?"

"No. I know this sounds strange, but my kids and I are going to be featured on a TV show regarding our experience living in a haunted house." When I heard myself say that, I thought, *Oh, great, this guy will surely think I'm crazy. Why did I say that?* I waited uncomfortably for his response.

Doug said in a kind, but curious voice, "I actually did a story on Ms. Johnson's disappearance years back. The case has always bothered me. I have always hoped there would be a resolution to the case, and that bastard, Hooker, would be charged with murder."

Then, to my surprise, Doug added, "If it takes a haunted house to bring that couple to justice, so be it! What can I do to help you?"

Relieved, I continued with my quest. "I would love to see the information you have regarding the entire story."

"There isn't a lot, and it's not our practice to keep things on file here. But a secretary a few years back had the foresight to keep a small file of old newspaper clippings regarding the missing girl. There are a few pictures of Madeline, Colleen, and the Hookers."

When I heard that Doug had a picture of the girl who had haunted my apartment, I almost passed out. I had researched with Lucy and Jenny on the internet, but had never found a photo or anything related to Madeline, other than the one reference to her disappearance during the Colleen Stan/Hookers trial.

Doug asked if I would like to make an appointment to see the clippings. After all the years of wondering what she looked like, I now had the opportunity to see if the girl in my dream was the same girl Hannah and I had been encountering from the spirit world.

My heart pounded and my thoughts raced as I said, "Yes, I would love to set up a time to see them." We made plans to meet in a couple of days. I hung up and then immediately called Jenny back to ask her to accompany me, and she agreed.

Night had arrived. Anticipation and excitement filled my mind. Images of what Madeline might look like dominated my thoughts. I wondered if the image I had seen in my visions would resemble the pictures in the paper, or if I had simply created them in my imagination. Young hippies from the seventies with flowers in their long hair were what I was conjuring. A rising winter wind and thunder roared outside. Simultaneously a storm was brewing inside my soul. I sat at my kitchen table sipping tea, deep in thought. I looked out my window at the dark storm, and every so often a cloud would move over the new moon, creating a silver pattern on the table in front of me. The past seven years had been a whirlwind of adventure and spiritual growth. I was finally going to see the face of my ghost, a captive sex slave, murdered, taken to a shallow grave somewhere in the mountains, and abandoned. I took in a deep breath, and started to weep uncontrollably, my heart beginning to break with the realization of just how many years had passed. My adventure had lasted seven years and Madeline's had been forgotten for decades.

Suddenly a clap of thunder roared, and rain started to pour outside, reminding me of tears. I thought of the drawings Hannah had given me a few years back. One drawing in particular was of an angel who she called "MyBelle."

I had kept it, and one other strange picture Hannah had drawn, safely tucked away in the back of my dream journal for seven years. I rushed to my bedroom, opened the top drawer to my nightstand, and grabbed the journal. I found the drawings in between my notes. As I held then in my hand looking down at them, shivers ran down my spine. I looked at the details of the angel, her flip hairdo, and the shirt she was wearing, so many details drawn by an innocent child. As I held onto the photos, my palms started to sweat, and I felt dizzy. It was though the red ink suddenly turned into the bloodstains of a murdered girl.

Morning arrived. I looked out my bedroom window as silent clouds drifted by; the storm had died down and the new day had a mystical and magical quality to it. Jenny and I were to meet Doug in an hour. Jenny arrived at my house promptly at nine a.m. It had started to rain again. As I ran out the door to her car, a howling sound echoed across the heavens. Thunder boomed, and rain poured down in buckets. As we drove, the rain danced on the roof of the car. It sounded like the buzzing of angry bees, yet at the same time, Jenny and I drove in a surreal silence. Before I knew it, we in the parking lot about to meet Doug for the first time.

While we were walking over to the front door, I realized that neither Jenny nor I had said a word to each other the entire time we drove, nor as we walked to the front door of the *Enterprise-Record*. Maybe it was the magic in the air. Maybe God wanted us to remain silent and meditate as we drove. Nonetheless, we were now going to see the face of the mysterious girl who haunted my apartment.

I recall my silent prayer: "God, help me to maintain my composure when I meet Doug. I don't want to lose it when I see her face, because I want to learn more about this long-forgotten mystery."

I looked over to Jenny and, as I opened the door for her to walk in before me, said, "It has been quite an interesting journey so far, don't you think?"

"Interesting, Jodi? That's putting it mildly. This has been one hell of an adventure, and you know what? I can't wait to see what happens next."

When I opened the door, the smell of newspaper and ink permeated the environment. I walked over to the reception desk.

"Hi, I have an appointment to meet with Doug Nelson."

"Have a seat. I will let him know you're here."

Five minutes passed before an older gentleman came over and said, "Hello, my name is Doug. You must be Jodi."

"Yes, I am Jodi, and this is my friend Jenny. She is my support person, since I am really nervous. I am so thankful that you took the time to meet with me."

He didn't waste any time. He said, "Jenny, grab your friend's hand, and follow me."

We were soon whisked into a conference room. "Go ahead and have a seat ladies. I'll be right back."

I watched Doug walk over to his desk, fiddle around for a few minutes, and shuffle through some files. He found what he was looking for and headed back to Jenny and me. In his hand, he held a dusty, old manila envelope. He sat in the chair across from us.

My legs started to shake. This was the moment—the moment I had anticipated for years. This would be the first time ever that I would see the face of my ghost. I could hardly contain myself. My mind raced. My heart felt as though it might jump out of my chest, as I sat anticipating what I would learn. I wondered, what would she look like? Would she resemble the girl from my visions and dreams? Would this finally be the confirmation I had waited for? The next few seconds seemed almost unbearable. I looked over to Jenny. I saw a small bead of sweat drip from her brow. She too was anxious, yet due to our silence, I hadn't realized it until now.

"Jenny, are you okay?" I asked.

"Are you?" she replied.

"Not really, but I have been waiting for a long time."

We both started laughing. The moment was surreal. Doug looked at us with a strange, yet amused look on his face. "It's not every day I have two beautiful ghost hunters in my office."

We all had a good laugh, and then I said, "Thank you for this opportunity. It really means more than you know."

Doug smiled. I watched as he carefully pulled the dusty thirty-year-old clippings from the manila envelope. Dust and the smell of old newspaper ink permeated the small conference room. I situated myself on the hard wooden chair and grabbed Jenny's hand. Our palms were both completely sweaty. I closed my eyes, took a deep breath, and said, "Okay Doug, I am ready to see the face of my ghost."

Doug unfolded one of the old papers, reached across the table, and handed me the article.

There she was: my ghost, I recognized her face; she was the girl from my nightmares. I gasped and felt a rush of adrenaline pump through me. The headline read "*Chicoan's Been Missing Five Years.*"

"Madeline Isabella Johnson, known to family and friends as, 'Maybelle'…"

"Oh my God, oh my God! It makes sense now Jenny, the name, it makes sense! Hannah's angel—'My Belle!' It finally makes sense! I can't believe it!" I exclaimed.

"What, Jodi? What about the name…what are you talking about?"

"Jenny, when we lived in the haunted apartment, Hannah used to say that her angel's name was MyBelle; Madeline's nickname is Maybelle!"

"Holy crap, Jodi, that's crazy!"

We stared at each other in awe at the realization. "Hannah really was talking to a ghost!"

I looked at Doug with tears in my eyes. "Thank you, Doug. Thank you so much. I finally have a face to put with all of my paranormal experiences—a beautiful face! She is an angel, just like Hannah said!"

I looked over at Jenny. She was trying to hold back her tears and excitement.

"Thank you Doug for letting two eccentric ladies into your office. You don't even know how this picture helps us."

Doug laughed curiously; I think he was amused by our bizarre story. "You know ladies, Maybelle's story has haunted me too, not in the same way as you gals, but haunted me nonetheless. I hope something comes out of your research, and that I have helped you."

"Thank you, Doug," I said with a tearful smile. "You have helped us so much. Really, there are no words to describe how much this helps me. Today you gave us a beautiful gift: the face of our ghost."

TWENTY-ONE

Wise Women and Girls

That night, I went to bed thinking about synchronicity and timing. Earlier, I read through the newspaper clippings Doug had given me, and noticed a strangely familiar date: February 20. I couldn't help but notice that today was actually February 20. As I continued to read through the papers, names, dates, and numbers seemed to jump off the pages at me. One in particular...February 1.

In a few hours, a crew from the A&E network was to arrive at my house to film a documentary about living in a haunted house and about being a child with clairvoyant abilities.

I prayed. "God, I appreciate the opportunity to be on TV with Hannah and to tell people about our haunting experience, but something about the timing seems off. Please help me to know how I should move forward."

That night, Wind Warrior appeared to me in a dream. He looked at me, never saying a word, just standing still and tall. I didn't understand the significance yet, but I understood this experience to be the sign I had prayed for.

The following day a famous psychic and psychologist along with a circus of people and cameras arrived at my house. Hannah had decorated her room in anticipation of the documentary, and we were all excited, especially to meet a famous psychic TV personality.

After we met the man, I was whisked off to the couch, off camera, to watch Hannah talk to the famous psychic. This man seemed nice; he asked Hannah if encountering paranormal activity as a child living in a haunted house frightened her. Hannah looked over at me and then to the psychic and with innocent eyes said; "No, I am not scared. The girl who was at my old house was just an angel. Why should I be scared of an angel?"

Again he asked, "Did she scare you? Did seeing a ghost scare you?"

Hannah replied, "No!" She looked over at me, confused, and then asked for a break.

She walked over to me and whispered in my ear, "Mom, I wasn't scared. Was I supposed to be?"

"Just speak your truth, honey," I told her. "The rest will fall into place."

She walked back into her beautiful, pink room and said, "I'm sorry, but I wasn't scared; I was lucky—lucky to see an angel. I'm not afraid. I just have a gift."

I was stunned that my child had such strength of character and was able to speak her mind about her feelings with such eloquence. Her confidence gave me strength to speak my truth.

I went over to the producer and said what I thought. "I really don't feel that this documentary is going in the right direction. I think that the documentary you're trying to make, and that wasn't made clear to us over the phone, is about *Psychic Intervention for Scared Children.* Hannah wasn't scared. It was the adults who were scared. Over the years, I've taught my kids not to be afraid of their experiences, but to ask and learn about the spiritual realm. When I was a kid, yes, I was scared. My mother didn't support me, nor did the fundamentalist Christian community that I grew up in, but I have made a conscious effort to support my children regarding unconventional spiritual issues, and we are not afraid. I actually thought that this was going to be about our family experience and me as a child."

"We've had a few meetings since our last conversation. This is our first episode, and we've decided to change the focus of the show to concentrate on psychic kids in crisis." The producer then said, "Let's take a break, so we can discuss what direction to take with your story."

After some discussion, the famous psychic and psychologist both came in to talk with me. The psychologist said,

"If we were doing a show about psychic moms, with psychic gifts as a child, this would have been great. However, the focus of our show is on helping kids in crisis today. We really like you and Hannah, but you're right. Neither of you need psychic intervention. You both seem to have psychic abilities, that's apparent, and you're both mentally healthy. Let's revisit doing a documentary in the near future."

I was thankful that a crew from A&E had come out to interview us and discuss our experience. I felt honored to have met famous TV personalities who agreed that Hannah and I were gifted. They were impressed with our courage to share our story. But we all knew that the timing wasn't right this time.

"Keep up the good work. I have the feeling that we will be seeing your story on the *big* screen in the future," the producer said.

"Thank you so much," I said. "This has been quite an education, and who knows, maybe we will work together in the future."

I felt a little let down that we hadn't had an opportunity to bring the story of Maybelle to light, but I soon would understand why, once again, timing and synchronicity were key.

One night shortly after the film crew left, I had a visitation from the spirit world. The visit was from a familiar soul who didn't manifest as a physical body, but rather as a smell of sweetly fragrant wildflowers and a feeling of kindness. The energy radiating from this soul was nonthreatening.

After a minute, I was able to ask the soul what it wanted and if I could help it in any way. I got a clear message. I was visually transported in my mind's eye to a remote location in a field with a small stream of water. I was standing behind a three-by-four-foot lava boulder. I heard a voice whisper in my ear, "35.76 miles northeast of Red Bluff." I looked down at the ground and could see a grayish-green land marker embedded in the dirt that read "A17."

I recognized the soft spirit, and she was asking for my help. "Jodi, please help me. There is a part to my story that needs to be brought to light; it's not just about me. There are other victims. Please be my voice."

Then I heard the name "Janice" whispered into my ear.

After I heard the name "Janice," I was confused and shaken. "Other victims, really?" I didn't know what that meant. "Could there be other victims of the Hookers?"

Thirty-plus years had passed since Maybelle had disappeared, and it didn't seem possible that, after all these years, the Hookers had gotten away with murder. "If there were other victims, who were they—and where are they?" Within seconds of the whisper, I was brought back into reality.

I recalled sitting at the kitchen table with Lucy and Jenny. We read a detailed account of Janice's arrangement with Cameron. He would be allowed sexual slaves, and she in exchange would have his babies. What kind of woman was she? What kind of mother helps her husband dispose of a body? Why was this woman roaming freely? My kids meant everything to me. I couldn't imagine exposing them to a father who was a murderer or sexual sadist.

I missed my children more than ever that night. Hannah and Sam were spending the night with friends. I was feeling lonely and confused, so I decided to call Lucy. She was a night owl, and I needed to talk.

She answered. "So you can't sleep either, huh?"

"Not really. I miss my kids. I just had this vivid vision and wanted to talk about it. Maybelle's spirit came to me—to let me know that something needs to be brought to light. I am not sure what it is yet, but the encounter got me thinking about Janice Hooker and other victims. What kind of woman gives her husband the opportunity to have a sexual slave in exchange for children? What kind of woman does something like that?"

"A sick and twisted woman," Lucy replied. "She probably got off on the idea of having a sexual slave, just like her husband. Come on, Jodi, she obviously had an agenda of her own: children, sex, and control. The woman is sick."

I was frustrated, and I started to cry. "So, do you think I let Maybelle down by not doing the documentary?"

"No, the timing wasn't right. Don't doubt your experience. Things happen in God's time, not ours."

"Hey, let's try to get our minds on something else. Why don't we go to lunch tomorrow and try to do some yard-sale shopping?"

"You're right. I need to get my mind off things."

We agreed to meet at the coffee shop at noon. The following day, after eating lunch, we set out on the town to locate a sale. Before long, we found ourselves at a small yard sale that looked interesting. The house was old, but well kept. The sun had been shining, and it was warm out. I got out of my car and started walking.

Lucy, a few steps behind me, said, "It feels like something weird is going to happen."

I brushed her off. "You're just jittery from all the coffee you drank."

We continued our walk over to some vintage clothing. As we started digging around, a young woman popped her head out from a flower garden and made her way over to us. While looking at the clothing, Lucy mentioned how beautiful the tiny house was and how the clothing fit into the decor.

The young woman laughed and said, "Yes, the clothes do have a vintage feel, although I was the one who designed and sewed them." She explained that she was moving to New York to go to design school and needed to get rid of some things before she went.

After a bit of small talk, I mentioned that I had recently had a TV crew from New York visit to do a documentary about me, my friends, and my daughter. Clearly intrigued, she asked about the subject matter.

"I know this is strange," I said, "but it was about living in a haunted apartment and an unsolved murder involving a man by the name of Cameron Hooker and his wife, Janice."

When I mentioned the names, she took a few steps back from me.

"Did I scare you?" I asked.

"No, you just surprised me," the young woman said. "My mother and I were just talking about these people last night. When will the documentary be out?"

"Well, actually, it's on hold for the time being."

"It's not a coincidence you're at this yard sale today," she said.

My heart started to race in anticipation, "What do you mean that this is no coincidence?" The young woman asked me and Lucy to have a seat on the bench next to her beautiful flower garden.

"What I am going to tell you is not supposed to be public information, but I think it might be of interest to you."

My palms started to sweat in anticipation.

She continued, "My mother works in the four-story building downtown at Fourth Street and Broadway. She came home upset the other day."

"Why?" I asked.

"According to my mom, there was a woman who was interested in renting the suite below her counseling office. Apparently, the woman was somehow connected to a national story involving a sex slave. Mom told me that the woman helped her husband abduct a young girl and, in fact, I think she said that the couple kept the woman locked in a coffin underneath their bed for something like seven years."

My stomach sank. Lucy looked over at me, perplexed.

"Counseling practice! What did you just say?...
Wait...wait a minute did you just say counseling office?"

I felt dizzy, yet somehow excited at the same time.

"Yes she is a counselor. Only a few people in the local
counseling community know her true identity, and my mom
is one of them."

Lucy got up off the bench and started pacing back and
forth. I sat trying to absorb this newfound information.
Signs, timing, and synchronicity. I thought.

The night before, I had talked with Lucy about my vision and wondered aloud: "Where does Janice Hooker live
and what does she do for a living?"

Lucy looked over at me and said, "Holy shit! Janice
Hooker is a freaking counselor!"

TWENTY-TWO

The Mysterious Woman

On June 4, Hannah's school was putting on a play at the local woman's club. Parents were invited to enjoy the play, along with music and food. Arriving that evening, I saw Heather, an acquaintance who also had a child in Hannah's class. Heather was petite with blond hair. She worked with abused women at a drug and alcohol program through the local hospital. Three months ago, while standing in line at the coffee shop to get pastries for the documentary crew, I found myself talking with Heather about the show and my paranormal adventure. I shared how it was connected to the infamous Cameron and Janice Hooker. Heather studied the case for a class she took in college, and knew about the sex slave story, but was appalled and disgusted to find out that they were also connected to an unsolved murder. At the end of our conversation, she asked me to get in touch with her to let her know how the documentary turned out, and when it would air on TV.

I had not seen Heather since our conversation in February, and I was a bit taken aback by her enthusiasm to see me tonight at the play. She rushed over and grabbed my arm.

"Jodi, I need to talk to you. Something has been weighing heavily on my mind. I have some information that might be of interest to you. It pertains to your paranormal experience. Have you finished filming yet?"

"Actually, some things happened, and we had to put the filming on hold, why?"

"A woman named Janice came into my office about an hour after I saw you at the coffee shop. She came into my office to interview for a counseling position. She had curly, light-brown, shoulder-length, highlighted hair, wore glasses, and was a bit plump—kind of dowdy, possibly in her late forties or early fifties. She didn't have any really striking facial features, but there was something odd about the woman…something strangely familiar, but I couldn't put my finger on it."

My legs started to buckle as I stood listening to her, I felt like I was going to have a panic attack. "Sorry, Heather. Please continue," I said, trying to remain steady on my feet.

"Her résumé stated that she had worked as an intern for the local county's mental-health program as an associate social worker from the years 2000 to 2007. She apparently worked for our program before, from 1997 through 2000. You know that our program deals with abused women and children. She also attended Chico State University, receiving straight As."

My thoughts raced as I remembered my recent vision, in which Maybelle had whispered in my ear, "Please help me."

Heather continued: "During the interview, Janice seemed uneasy, staring off into the distance and never making eye contact. At first, I thought this behavior might be just nerves, since interviewing is never easy. But that wasn't it—she still had a disconnected demeanor even an hour into the interview. This is a position working with abused and addicted women; connection and empathy are imperative."

As Heather continued talking, my heart raced, and I felt a panic attack coming on. I called out to Ted, who was talking to some friends only a few steps away.

"Hey, Ted, can you come here for a second? I want you to listen to this story with me." Ted and I had been separated for a while, but we continued to co-parent the kids. He continued to support me in my quest to find justice for Madeline.

"Is everything okay?" he replied.

"Well, I am not sure. Heather is telling me a story, and I want another ear to hear this along with me." I whispered in his ear, "Ted, I feel a panic attack coming on. I need you to stand here with me."

"No problem," he told me. "Hi, Heather. It's nice to see you," he offered before putting his arm around me.

Heather continued: "There was something odd about Janice, but I couldn't put my finger on it. I was so concerned that I decided to end the interview. I told Janice that I would hand her paperwork to the next administrative interviewer, and they would be in touch.

"I kept going over the interview in my head," Heather continued, "asking myself, *Why would this woman, Janice, who seemingly has nothing wrong with her, make me feel so disturbed?* All of a sudden, I figured it out—the woman I had interviewed for the counseling position was none other than the infamous Janice Hooker!"

The infamous Janice Hooker. My stomach sank at her words. I looked over to Ted. He was in shock. His eyes were as round as saucers, and he said, "Are you kidding me? Janice Hooker is a counselor in our community!" This was the second time in a few days that I heard Janice Hooker was a counselor. And the first time I heard she was working with woman and children.

"Heather, are you sure it is her, and not another Janice?" I was trying not to cry. A rush of adrenaline ran through my body. Ted held on to my hand as she continued to talk.

"Yes, I am sure. I got on my computer and did a search for Janice Hooker. There she was—the same woman I had interviewed earlier, staring back at me. But Janice was no longer using the last name Hooker. She had a different last name."

Ted asked, "So you're telling us that she has been a social-worker intern, working with people in crisis...with mentally ill and abused women—and in Chico?"

"Good God!" I yelled. "The woman who helped her husband capture a sex slave and murder Madeline Johnson is working in the mental-health community!"

"Yes!" Heather said. "I immediately went to my supervisor. But get this: my supervisor wasn't shocked. She knew of Janice and her involvement with two different counseling organizations. She told me that there had been quite a scandal involving many higher-ups in the hospital administration. See, Jodi, our program is associated with the hospital. After finding out that Janice worked as an intern, people at the hospital were advised to keep quiet, or they would lose their jobs."

Suddenly, I was brought back to the reality of being in a crowded room—a room filled with young kids bustling around, getting ready for a school play. I had been so engrossed by Heather's story that I had forgotten we were at a social gathering. I could feel my legs shaking and my heart racing. Feeling dizzy, I gripped Ted's hand tightly. I tried to maintain my composure.

Heather then said, "There is more disturbing information. Janice worked at the local county's mental-health program as an intern during the year 2000—the same year you lived at the apartment complex—and she was one of the intake workers for the inpatient unit. People who felt suicidal, schizophrenics; people with depression and anxiety met her first."

The local county's mental-health program was a half a block away from my old apartment—the haunted apartment! Madeline's apartment!

"Good God!" I exclaimed. "The mentally ill, abused, and addicted people are unaware that they are in the care and presence of an accomplice to murder! This woman helped her husband kidnap Colleen Stan and hold her for seven years as a sexual slave. She helped her husband dispose of Madeline's remains. It's no wonder the apartment had paranormal activity!"

I looked at Ted and said, "Oh my God, when I lived in the apartment and experienced such horrendous paranormal activities, Jenny encouraged me to go there for counseling. I actually called to make an appointment but couldn't get in for a month. The lady said if it were a dire emergency that I should go to their inpatient unit. Oh my God!"

I looked at Ted and Heather and said, "It makes me sick to think that a person could penetrate the very environment of the innocent. Oh my God! Oh my God! Ted, she worked on the same street, the very street, where she and her husband abducted Maybelle! Now I understand why our apartment was being haunted. Maybelle needed to get someone's attention. She needed someone to see, and understand that her murderer was only a half a block away, working with the mentally ill!"

I realized that the haunting hadn't been about me, Hannah, Jenny, or Jessica. It had been bigger. It had been about justice. Maybelle had died—but in death, she had a mission. She wanted to warn the innocent about a master manipulator.

After making it through the school play feeling dazed and emotionally exhausted, I went home to prepare for Sam's birthday the following day. Ted came with me. I told him that I really didn't want to be alone after what we had just learned.

At home, I decided to grab a cup of tea and go out to sit on my porch swing. Ted stayed inside and got the kids ready for bed. As I sat on the swing, I took a few deep breaths to try and calm my nerves. I tried to make sense of everything I just learned. Concern after concern flooded my heart and soul. Janice, according to what I had read from newspaper reports and in *The Perfect Victim,* was portrayed as a person with low intelligence and low self-esteem. I couldn't help but wonder how she could make it through school and attain a master's degree, let alone get straight As? But the most terrifying thought of all—if I had actually needed to go to the mental hospital's inpatient unit, my intake worker would have been the infamous Janice Hooker.

I had been so deeply affected by what Heather said that I had lost track of time. Eventually, I realized that Ted and the kids were all sleeping. I was still on the front porch swing, in shock. I looked into the house to see what time it was—almost midnight. As I sat on the swing, an overwhelming sense of loss over came me, and I started to cry. Sam woke up when he heard me weeping. I saw him walking towards me with a silver music box in his hand. He had turned it on and it was playing a sweet lullaby. "Hi honey, I am really sorry I woke you up. I was thinking about family and friends that I haven't seen for a while. I was thinking about my mother."

Sam sat next to me and said, "Mommy, open your hand. This heart is from your mom. She told me to give it to you when I was sleeping." I never talked about my mom with Sam, so it struck me as especially odd.

"Thank you, honey. Why were you thinking of my mom?" Sam had never met her, and I never had any pictures of her, so Sam talking about her was extremely strange.

"Mommy, she woke me up to tell me to give you this heart, and then she left."

"Wow, Sam, that is really nice. Thank you so much, honey. You should get to bed. Tomorrow is your birthday, and we have a lot to do."

Sam wiped his sleepy five-year-old eye, hugged me, then went back to bed. "I love you, Mama. Good night."

I was exhausted. Sam's birthday was tomorrow and the situation with Janice weighed heavily on my mind. I held on to the silver heart and for a brief moment thought about the last time I had been with my mom, which, simultaneously, made me think of the last time Madeline talked to her family. I felt, in that moment at five minutes after midnight, that I needed to go deep into my heart and ask God for special and specific guidance. So I did.

I decided to make a circle of salt on my living room floor. I rummaged through an old dresser in my bedroom and found a white candle along with some white sage. I lit them both and placed them, along with a red rose Sam had picked for me earlier, in a blue ceramic bowl in the center.

I called out to God: "I need a vision; I need direction and answers."

I lay in the circle with my eyes closed. I soon found myself chanting a Native American song. While chanting, I could hear a distant drum. I continued to chant, going deeper and deeper into a meditative trance.

During my trance, I was transported to a familiar place in the mountains. I recognized the location; it was the open meadow next to my childhood home. I was sitting next to a fire pit. When I looked across, I saw Wind Warrior. He smiled and acknowledged my presence with a nod of his head. When he did, I noticed two feathers beautifully interwoven into his long braids. I watched as he untied them. He reached over towards me and placed one in my right hand and one in my left hand, while continuing to look straight into my eyes.

"These feathers represent two souls," he said, "souls that are connected through many lifetimes to each other."

He then motioned to the east with a small wave of his hand and quietly said, "It is the vision you asked for."

I looked over to the east. There was a creek, and I could see two women sitting and talking. Upon looking closer, I recognized them. One was Colleen Stan. The other was Janice Hooker. I looked back over at Wind Warrior. I felt anger boiling inside of me.

"I don't understand," I said.

Wind Warrior looked at me sternly and said, "Observe!"

I did what he asked. While observing, I could hear the women negotiating.

I heard Janice say to Colleen, "Let's remain friends; no one else will understand our experience. You helped raise my kids. Colleen, I know you don't want them to suffer. I know I was hard on you in the beginning, and I used you as a slave. But things have evolved. And I still love you and Cameron."

During their conversation, Janice manipulated Colleen, avowing her undying devotion because they shared the common thread of torture.

Janice then said, "Please understand, I want my family to remain intact. The children need to be with their family, and your agreement to remain quiet about your enslavement would ensure their safety. Cameron has changed; he wants us all to be happy. He is sorry for what he did to you."

"Ma'am," Colleen said, "I am afraid Cameron will hurt the girls when they are older. Do you really think he has changed? Why, after all these years, are you letting me go?"

Janice replied, "Cameron talked to me about having a child with you, but you see, this would break our original agreement. Years ago, we agreed that he could have sexual slaves. In exchange, I would remain the first wife: the one in charge, and the only one to bear his children. I am the one who decided to let you go. It's time for you to start your own life. Cameron understands."

"Yes, ma'am, I understand. Thank you for letting me out of my contract," Colleen replied.

After hearing this, I was furious. I had witnessed true victimization during my vision. I saw Janice in true form, a master at manipulating. During the vision, Colleen seemed passive and in agreement, thinking not of herself but only of the Hooker children. I could see clearly Colleen's kind and thoughtful soul.

I looked back over to Wind Warrior, still feeling furious. "How is observing this conversation going to help me or anyone else?"

Wind Warrior reached over to me; I could see he was holding a medicine bag in his hand.

"Hold out your left hand," he said before placing the medicine bag into my palm. I looked at it for a minute. It was beautiful, and strangely familiar. The energy emanating from it resonated with strength and peace. Somehow it made me want to cry, so I placed it next to my heart. I recognized it. It was the medicine bag that my mother had made for my ninth birthday—the same day my beloved grandfather had died.

As I held the bag close to my heart, I remembered the story my mom had told me when she presented it to me:

"Jodi, I killed the deer myself, tanned the hide, and sewed two beautiful crystals to the front of the medicine bag. The two crystals represent two souls that will eternally be connected—yours and mine. It holds your magic. The deer that sacrificed its life gave us its magic. Now, over your lifetime, put your own magic into it."

I cried, thinking about the last time I had seen my mother. It wasn't a good memory. It was a horrible memory of being kicked out in the cold Montana snow while sick and of feeling alone with Hannah. I had not yet reconciled with my Hermie, even after many, many years. She was almost a distant memory of someone else's life, not mine.

While I sat crying, I heard Wind Warrior say, "Look up at me, Jodi." I could see he was looking across the fire pit over my right shoulder. He said, "Jodi, you have a guardian. She lives in the spirit world with me now." I started to tremble; I felt chills run through my soul. In the clearing behind me was a woman standing in the old pasture. It was Hermie. She smiled, walked over to me, and then reached out her hand. I put my hand in hers. Her eyes sparkled like crystal. She sat next to me at the fire pit, holding my hand.

Wind Warrior said, "Hermie is in the spirit world now. She passed alone in a cabin in Montana with bone cancer. Your little sister Michelle tried to save her, but it was too late."

I cried and said, "Hermie, Hermie...No!"

He spoke for my mother: "Your mother is sorry for all the pain she caused you during her lifetime."

Mom reached over and put her arms around me. She whispered in my ear, "Jodi, I am sorry for abandoning you. I did the best I could. You have many gifts and talents, and I am proud of you! You are a strong and mighty woman— go and tell your story, the story of the haunted apartment, the story of Madeline Isabella Johnson. When you do, people will become aware and enlightened. Reach into your medicine bag; inside are the answers."

We all have a medicine bag inside our soul. It is there from the birth of your soul...it is your God-given gift to access and use. Don't let religion or dogma tell you what is right or wrong. You were born with a gift! Hold onto the gift, access your gifts to serve humankind, and know that there is a higher realm of existence always guiding your steps. Be a voice for those who are weak and weary or lost, sing a song, hold a hand, give from the heart, and love with our resistance. You never know when fate will intervene, and sometimes what looks or feels like a horrible thing might simply be a matter of perception.

At one point in my life, I had thought living in a haunted house was a horrible experience. But now things had changed. I was guided by a supernatural force—be it from Maybelle, Wind Warrior, or my mom. Though many years had passed, justice still needed to be served. I sat reflecting back on past experiences, such as living in a haunted apartment, and having paranormal encounters as a child, and thought:

God, angels, and passed-on loved ones can intervene when the timing is right—and I knew it in the pit of my stomach, just as my grandfather the mortician had said so many years before.

The time was right for me to assist in the cold case of Madeline Isabella Johnson.

TWENTY-THREE

My Mother (Hermie)

I mourned the loss of my mother. I was also in shock from learning about Janice Hooker. I was experiencing a plethora of feelings and emotions. Thank God Ted and the kids were with me. He called Lucy and Jenny to let them know I had just experienced a tragedy. The gals rushed to my side and supported me through my grief. I didn't know if I would be able to handle anything, so my friends stepped in to help with the kids and meals. I was extremely distraught because I had many unresolved issues with my mom. I did, however, feel blessed that she had made her way to me in the spirit realm.

A week passed. I continued to mourn. I didn't know what to do.

"Why don't you give your sister a call?" Ted said. "You can ask her what she is going to do regarding your mom's memorial service."

"Ted, I am afraid my siblings don't understand me. They kicked me out of their lives years ago. Whenever I attempted to contact them, they weren't receptive."

"Try again," Ted said. "It's never too late, Jodi, and I am sure your mom would want you to connect with them now."

He was right. My sister and my mom had remained close. I knew she would be the one to take care of all the funeral arrangements. I called, and Michelle answered the phone.

"Hi, Michelle. This is your sister Jodi. Are you okay? It's good to hear your voice. It's been so many years since we've talked. I'm so sorry, so, so sorry, about Mom. I can't believe Hermie's gone. She was only fifty-nine."

Right then it dawned on me that both Hermie and my grandpa had both passed at the age of fifty-nine, and that both had passed on birthdays. Grandpa died on my ninth birthday, and my mom died on Sam's sixth birthday. It was surreal.

"Not good, but I am really glad you called. I know we have all had our differences, but I want you to know that Hermie was thinking about you a lot before she died. While she lay in my arms, she said, 'Please tell Jodi I am proud of her.'"

Holding back tears, I said, "I know this sounds weird, but I'm calling because Hermie came to me in a dream to let me know she died."

Michelle cried, then said, "Hermie wanted to be cremated. She told me to take her ashes and scatter them in the mountains where she and her horse would ride. She wanted each one of us kids to have our own intimate service near a creek or mountain, alone with her spirit."

My mom had been a very private person, and this kind of intimate ceremony fit her personality and quirks perfectly. Michelle and I cried on the phone, talking for hours about life, kids, and Hermie. The conversation ended with Michelle saying, "Jodi, remember when we were kids, and you had a panic attack? I think you were about twelve. Well, I told Hermie the next day about how you snuck into her bedroom. She told me that she knew you were there and that she felt you touch your finger to hers. It was hard for her to show emotions Jodi—so, so hard. She was too proud to let you know that she was there for you."

I cried throughout the night as I held my kids and Ted. And as day started to break the following day, I decided to have my intimate memorial with my mother. There was a special spot near the creek at One Mile in Bidwell Park. It was a perfect place to remember, celebrate, and honor Hermie's life. I packed a small basket: old pictures, a white candle, some sage, a small bottle of whiskey, her brand of tobacco, and the magical gift of the medicine bag that had been given to me as a nine-year-old girl. I also packed some fried chicken in memory of the first meal I had made for her as a child. (I wasn't able to find fried rabbit!)

When I got to the spot next to the creek, I laid out a blanket. The sun shone, and the creek flowed gently. I sat down on the blanket with the basket full of memories arranged nicely next to me.

I took in a deep breath; the smoky hide scent from the medicine bag I was wearing around my neck reminded me of Hermie. I prayed, "Mom, thank you for giving me life, and life lessons. I am thankful for all the experiences I was able to share with you. I am sorry we didn't talk after that horrible winter day in Montana. I forgive you and myself. Please rest in the loving arms of God. I love you. I will miss you."

After the prayer, I took a swig of the whiskey and a bite of the fried chicken to honor her spirit. I cried and moaned. The loss and emptiness I felt was almost unbearable.

I thought about how memorials gave the living the chance to honor, remember, and grieve. The ceremony I had created to honor my mom made me wonder if Madeline Isabella Johnson's family had ever been able to grieve their loss or memorialize and honor Maybelle's life.

As I lay in the sun, it occurred to me: not only had May-belle wanted me to know about Janice Hooker's involvement in the counseling community, but she had wanted to be acknowledged as well—as a sister, a lover, a friend, and a daughter. I remembered back to how the apartment had been blessed by the neighborhood church and how Jenny and I had done a prayer and ritual to send Maybelle to God. What we hadn't done was acknowledge her as a living being. This new understanding gave me an idea. However, I first had to do some more research.

I spent the next couple of hours honoring my mom and thinking about how she was now able to help me as a spirit in a way she never could when she was alive.

TWENTY-FOUR

Taking a Wrong Turn... Turns Out to Be the Right Turn

M y mother's passing inspired me to continue learning about Madeline Isabella Johnson. My clairvoyant abilities convinced that me she had never had a formal memorial service, but I needed concrete evidence. The only information I had so far was from the research the girls and I had done on the computer some time back and the newspaper articles Doug Nelson of the *Enterprise-Record* had given us. Other than her photo and my memories of her haunting my apartment, I didn't have much to go on.

I couldn't help but wonder who she was. I went to my room and took out my journal and the newspaper clippings.

I sat at my kitchen table with a cup of tea, looking everything over.

The photos from the newspaper portrayed a pretty, young girl with green eyes and a beautiful smile. I pored over one article from 1981; "Chicoan's Been Missing Five Years," which read something like, "Where is Madeline Isabella Johnson? She is 5'5" and 110 pounds, with brown hair and green eyes. Chico police have been trying to answer that question for five years. A private investigator, a psychic, the FBI, and even an African witch doctor have looked into the case."

I was shocked to read that a psychic and a witch doctor had been used.

I continued reading. "Chico detectives routinely screen all bulletins of Jane Does that meet Johnson's physical characteristics. Flyers about the missing woman have been sent to police agencies throughout the county. Miss Johnson's family enlisted the aid of a psychic. The psychic gave a Chico location, where the police searched and came up with nothing. A foster son of one of the family's relatives showed her picture to a witch doctor. The witch doctor warned the person to stay out of the situation. Maybelle's father, a businessman from Cleveland, Ohio, said, 'She telephoned her mother the night before she disappeared, saying she had become disenchanted with California and wanted help in going to school in Ohio. But she had written a friend in Ohio on January 30, 1976, only two days before she disappeared, saying things were going well with her boyfriend and they were planning on getting married after she got her paralegal degree.'"

As I read on, the report said that "Maybelle was not into narcotics, religious cults, or terrorist organizations. Although she did object to some things at home, Johnson stressed he and his daughter were close. And in fact, in a letter written the night before she disappeared, she wished her mother a happy birthday and expressed a passion and love for her mother, saying, 'I really mean what I say when I tell you that you are the most wonderful mother in the world. Even though I have always been very close to you and we did everything for each other, I unintentionally hurt you and Dad, the most important and closest people to me. But you are still giving me much-wanted and appreciated advice and much encouragement. I have some modeling jobs set up for a couple of downtown Chico clothing stores. I am looking forward to working and making some money. I love you and Dad so much and will talk to you soon.'"

Chills ran down my spine, and I started to shake. Realization rushed through me like a bolt of lightning. The name stood out from the newspaper. *Oh, my God...I understand now! Hannah's coveted Ernie doll, the one who screamed, "I feel great!" three times, shared the same name as Maybelle's father. She was trying to communicate her father's name to me—she wanted him to know she hadn't forgotten him or her mother!*

I took a deep breath and read the end of the newspaper clipping. Johnson begged for a favor, saying, "Everyone misses her terribly. Please help us bring our baby home!"

I continued reading. Another clipping from December 20, 1984, read, "Sex slave suspect linked to Chico kidnapping. A Red Bluff man and his wife are suspected in the slaying and disappearance of a missing woman from Chico named Madeline Isabella Johnson. Janice Hooker, after what she called a 'religious awakening,' confessed to a pastor from the Nazarene Church that she, her husband, and Colleen Stan were in a relationship similar to that of Sarah and Hagar in the Bible. During this admission, she confessed that she and Cameron had abducted, slain, and buried a missing Chico woman. The police took her confession seriously and notified the family, even though they had never been able to locate Maybelle's remains."

The newspaper clippings were horrifying. I felt frustrated and sick that after thirty-plus years, there had still been no resolution. Now that I had the name of Maybelle's father, I decided to see if I could locate him.

After a few futile computer searches, I came across someone who might be related to Maybelle. After finding the name and a phone number, I wasn't sure what to do. *Should I call or write? How would I react if someone contacted me after all these years, saying, "Hi, I lived in a haunted apartment, and your dead sister tried to contact me. I was wondering if you were ever able to give her a memorial."*

I really started to understand the magnitude of the emotions surrounding Maybelle's disappearance and the multitude of clues I had been given over the years. Things were starting to make sense.

I sat at the table, looking through my journal and newspaper in contemplation, when all of a sudden something I had written down in my journal stood out. I had written down the name of a road and mileage: "35.76 miles northeast of Red Bluff, California, on road A17." *Could this be the possible location of Madeline Isabella Johnson? I had information that could potentially help solve a mystery.*

I decided to write down everything I knew: dates, times, names, locations. I laid out the details from my dream journal, newspaper clippings, and the internet to the best of my ability. The pieces of a mysterious puzzle seemed to be coming together into what looked like potentially helpful information. Everything seemed in order, but something was still missing. Something still wasn't quite right.

At the time, I didn't know what the nagging feeling was, and I didn't identify it until later that day when Hannah had a play date with a girlfriend.

While I sat at the kitchen table reviewing the papers lying everywhere, trying to make sense of things, Hannah came over and said, "Hey, Mom, my friend Christine just called. She wants me to come over to visit. Is that okay?"

"Sure, honey. Let me put these papers away, and then I will drive you over." I thought a change of scenery would help me clear my thoughts.

Hannah's friend lived across town with her stepmother, who worked for the Chico Police Department. I had a few errands to run, so I said to Hannah, "Come with Mommy to do errands, and after we're done, I'll drop you off."

We headed out the door. While driving back from errands, I accidentally drove down the wrong end of the street where Hannah's friend lived. When I rounded the corner, I felt a sense of impending doom. My stomach started to ache, and I felt as if I were going to pass out. I felt a panic attack coming on, but I couldn't figure out why. I wondered if it was the stress of looking over all the newspaper clippings or the fact that I had recently lost my mother. My heart started to race, and I felt nauseated.

Hannah was in the front seat. She looked over at me and said, "Mommy, are you okay?"

"No, honey," I said, "I feel like throwing up." My heart continued to race. My mouth was dry. I was scared! I needed to pull over immediately. Somehow, I found myself stopped two doors down from Hannah's friend's house. I decided to get out of my car to try to catch my breath.

"Mommy, Mommy, are you okay?"

Tears flowed down my cheeks. I yelled at Hannah, "No, no, I am not okay! Mommy feels sick!"

When I yelled, I looked up and over to the right. I noticed a woman standing in her front yard. She had light, shoulder-length hair and wore glasses. She looked to be around fifty years old. The woman stood there staring at me. She didn't rush to my side to see if I was okay. She didn't look concerned that I was crying, or parked next to her driveway. The woman only stared at me. I stared back with tear-filled eyes, wondering why she didn't come over to see if I was okay. I stood with beads of sweat pouring from my brow and my heart beating hard. I was in a full-blown panic attack.

I remember thinking, as I looked at the woman and cried, that she looked strangely familiar. I knew her! I knew who the woman was! I recognized her from my dreams. I recognized this woman deep in my soul. *It's Janice Hooker*—the infamous Janice Hooker! She was standing in her yard staring at me. I couldn't believe my eyes! She looked the same, just like photos I had seen before, only older, with shorter blond hair.

All I could think was, *No freaking way! No freaking way!*

Not only had Janice Hooker penetrated the counseling community, she also lived two freaking doors down from someone who works at the police department!

I wanted to run over to her, tackle her to the ground, and beat her silly until she felt the pain of Maybelle and the pain of Colleen.

All of the fear, rage, confusion, and horror I had experienced in the haunted apartment rushed to the surface. I wanted to yell, "You are guilty! You are guilty! You're a kidnapper, a rapist, and a murderer, just like your husband! Do you really think you are going to get away with this and not be responsible for your crimes because you were manipulative and smart? Becoming a counselor does not redeem you or make you a free woman! You will pay for your crimes! *You will pay!*"

I felt the rage of a murdered girl; I felt the rage and sadness of Maybelle and Colleen. I felt my own sadness and pain. I felt mad that my child and my friends had experienced terror and confusion while we lived in the haunted apartment.

Janice stared at me while I stood there having an anxiety attack. All I could think was; *Hold it together, Jodi. Hold it together! Don't run and tackle her to the ground!* I told myself, *now you know Janice Hooker's location!* I remember taking in a deep breath and then looking up to the mailbox next to me. I saw Janice Hooker's new last name.

Without a shadow of a doubt, this was the last clue I needed before I could put all my information together.

"Mom, are you okay?" Hannah yelled from the car.

"Yes, honey! Yes! I am okay!"

I got back into my car. I looked over at Hannah and then said, "Mommy just found a missing piece to a puzzle. I'm really sorry that I yelled at you."

I knew that landing on Janice's doorstep hadn't been a coincidence. It had all been orchestrated with perfect timing. Only hours before, when I had been reviewing journals and documents, I had a nagging feeling in the pit of my stomach. Something had been missing, and I then understood what it was. I had been led by all of my spiritual helpers to the exact location of Janice Hooker. In my heart, I knew this wasn't the end. It was a beginning!

With my newfound information, I went home to write Janice a letter.

Dear Janice,

I felt compelled to write you a letter. I pray you will go deep into your heart and soul to understand that you need to help resolve an issue from thirty-plus years ago. I moved from Montana to Chico with my daughter in 1999. When I got to Chico, I was looking for affordable housing. I was lucky enough to find an affordable apartment on the north end of town. An address I suspect you are well aware of.

I felt happy and blessed to find such a nice place and neighbors. Upon moving into the apartment on February 1, 2000, my daughter, my friends, and I all started to have strange nightmares and experiences. I asked God to help me understand the reasons for such strange occurrences. God answered my prayers and directed me to you. In fact, he directed me to your exact location!

There is a family who lost their daughter because of what you and your ex-husband did in 1976. You admitted that your husband murdered Madeline Isabella Johnson, and you helped him take her remains to a remote, mountainous location and buried her in a shallow grave. Her family lost their sister, child, and loved one.

In 1984, you supposedly took law enforcement to where you thought her burial site was, but then said that due to time and stress, you had forgotten the exact location. I believe that you lied about the location. You are a mother, a counselor, and, from what I understand, a Christian. The spirit world knows the truth, Janice.

Sincerely,
Jodi Foster

After writing the letter to Janice, I felt a plethora of emotions flooding my soul: sadness, rage, and anger. I questioned whether I should take the letter to her house or send it though the mail. If I took the letter myself, I might want to punch her straight in the face and rip out her hair. Clearly, I had been directed to Janice's exact location for a reason. But was it in order to give her a letter and punch her in the face? Probably not such a good idea! I decided it would be best if I called Jenny immediately, before I did something completely irrational. I knew Jenny was going to be shocked that I found Janice, but maybe together, we could come up with a more rational plan than pulling Janice's hair out.

When I got in touch with Jenny, I said, "You're not going to believe this! I was driving Hannah to her friend's house when, all of a sudden, I found myself miraculously at the exact location of Janice Hooker!"

"No freaking way, Jodi! No freaking way!" Jenny screamed. I heard Jenny drop the phone. I wondered if she had passed out or was immediately running over to my house.

"Jenny, are you there?" I yelled.

I heard her laughing and screaming. "Yes! Yes! Good God, it's a miracle!" The phone lay on the floor until finally she grabbed it. Shocked and barely able to get a word out, she said, "There is no freaking way you found Janice Hooker."

"Without a shadow of doubt, it was her, Jenny! I saw her. It was definitely her! I know where she lives!

"Jenny," I continued, "I wrote her a letter, and I wanted to take it to her doorstep."

"Jodi, are you nuts? Don't do it! Aren't you afraid?"

"Yes, I'm afraid, and most likely nuts as well. But Jenny, I know I have to do something!"

"Wait for me," Jenny said. "Don't go anywhere. I will be right there. Don't move!"

Jenny arrived at my house about ten minutes later with a mischievous look in her eyes. I thought to myself, *Great, we have both gone insane. Jenny is supposed to be my voice of reason.*

I remember sitting on my living room floor, shaking, holding the letter tightly in my hand. I kept thinking that Janice and Cameron Hooker had gotten away with their deranged and twisted plan for more than thirty years now. I wondered, *Could a letter from me make a difference? Will my letter remind her of how she intentionally brainwashed*

Colleen Stan and served as an accomplice to Maybelle's murder?
I wanted Janice to remember that a higher power was still
watching her…and so was the spirit of Madeline Isabella
Johnson.

Though many years had passed, justice still needed to
be served. I sat, pondering whether I should take or send
the letter. I reflected back on past experiences, such as living
in a haunted apartment, having paranormal encounters as
a child, and finally put together the numerous pieces to a
long-forgotten mystery. I knew what my next move would
be. It was clear as crystal.

I took in a deep breath, held Jenny's hand, and said, "I
know what I have to do."

With Jenny and Ted by my side, I grabbed the phone
and dialed the Chico Police Department.

With conviction in my voice, I said, "I am not sure who
I should talk to, but I am calling in regard to a cold case
from thirty-plus years ago. It involves a girl by the name of
Madeline Isabella Johnson."

I soon found myself connected to a detective by the
name of Bill Smith, and went on to tell my story in its entirety. Detective Smith was skeptical, yet open to new information and willing to listen to my wild tale. After I had
laid out all the details, he said, "It's not every day I receive a
phone call like yours. I do know of this case, and it has been
a mystery for many years. Your story is quite intriguing, but
you will have to understand my skepticism."

I replied, "I completely understand your skepticism, and I, too, was skeptical—at one time."

Before I knew it, I was catapulted into an unfamiliar world. I was sitting with detectives and FBI agents who asked me to draw maps and to explain every detail regarding the coordinates of where I believed Maybelle's remains might be. I was asked to describe my experiences and encounters with the paranormal. I was asked to describe the people, places, and things I had seen in my nightmares. I described every detail I could remember. The meeting lasted for hours. After gleaning every bit of information possible, detective Smith thanked me, shook my hand, turned, and said, "Jodi, sometimes God works in mysterious ways."

Epilogue

Maybelle Johnson, without a shadow of doubt, reached out to me from beyond the grave. I heard her cries.

I now understand that I am a clairvoyant, empath, and a sensitive. I accept these gifts and use them to the best of my abilities to help those in need. Maybelle was much more than a beautiful girl; she was my teacher and a beautiful soul.

The case is currently an active murder investigation in the hands of the Red Bluff Police Department. Due to the sensitive nature of the case, the police asked me to remain quiet about my experience—until it could be prosecuted. The police are currently in the process of bringing Maybelle's case to justice.

There is a verse in the Bible that helped me to understand my incredible experiences: "To everything there

is a season, and time to every purpose under heaven."
(Ecclesiastes 3:1)

The paranormal adventure with Madeline Isabella
Johnson is not over yet. There are many other people
involved in this incredible multilayered sex slave, murder mystery. And as in the verse above, when the time
is right, more will be revealed. I will soon be able to
share with you what happened next to all involved, as
the story is still unfolding.

This story is a memorial and testament to the sur-
vival of spirit and consciousness.

Maybelle now has a voice, and will never be forgotten!